# COACH:

# A Safety Leadership Fable

SHAWN M. GALLOWAY

**SCE Press**

Copyright © 2023 Shawn M. Galloway

All Rights Reserved

ISBN: 979-8-9873873-0-6

For my wife.

My Lucy.

# Contents

| | |
|---|---|
| INTRODUCTION | 6 |
| CHAPTER ONE *The Bare-Knuckle Bunch* | 8 |
| CHAPTER TWO *Culture Clash!* | 12 |
| CHAPTER THREE *"Do as I Say, Not as I Say"* | 18 |
| CHAPTER FOUR *The Clueless Supervisor* | 23 |
| CHAPTER FIVE *Search for a Coach* | 28 |
| CHAPTER SIX *There's More to Safety Than Safety* | 34 |
| CHAPTER SEVEN *Who's in Charge of This Jungle?* | 38 |
| CHAPTER EIGHT *Just Use It!* | 45 |
| CHAPTER NINE *A Very Frustrated "Monk of Mention"* | 50 |
| CHAPTER TEN *A Treasured Visit* | 55 |
| CHAPTER ELEVEN *A STEP Forward?* | 58 |
| CHAPTER TWELVE *It's Not About the Pizza!* | 62 |
| CHAPTER THIRTEEN *Now What?* | 66 |
| CHAPTER FOURTEEN *Heartbreak* | 71 |
| CHAPTER FIFTEEN *Learning to Lead by Coaching* | 76 |
| CHAPTER SIXTEEN *Battling Snakes of Different Sorts* | 80 |
| CHAPTER SEVENTEEN *What Does Success Look Like?* | 87 |
| CHAPTER EIGHTEEN *Let's Go with the Pizza!* | 93 |
| CHAPTER NINETEEN *No Monk Injured on My Watch!* | 99 |
| CHAPTER TWENTY *No More Charts, No More Metrics* | 104 |
| CHAPTER TWENTY-ONE *Who, Me? Really?* | 109 |
| CHAPTER TWENTY-TWO *Alpha, Solophant and Me, Plus Phil* | 115 |
| CHAPTER TWENTY-THREE *Shall We Dance?* | 122 |
| CHAPTER TWENTY-FOUR *Posterior for Posterity?* | 127 |
| CHAPTER TWENTY-FIVE *Rump Pizza and an "Innovation of Interest"* | 135 |
| CHAPTER TWENTY-SIX *North, Short, Shady, and Berry* | 139 |
| CHAPTER TWENTY-SEVEN *And Finally, Facilitation* | 145 |
| CHAPTER TWENTY-EIGHT *Pilot? Visionary?* | 152 |
| ABOUT THE AUTHOR | 156 |

# INTRODUCTION

Many years ago, at a refinery, days away from recognizing three years without a recordable injury, a terrible thing happened. A supervisor walking down some stairs within operations heard something squeak. Even though the contract with the labor union stated that management is supposed to direct rather than perform work, he found and picked up an oil can. He opened an access door to identify the source of the noise, bypassing a lockout-tagout procedure. Leaning in, now off-balance, he placed his left hand on a steel rod to stabilize himself. As the rod abruptly dropped down around a piece of machinery, it immediately amputated four fingers.

For multiple reasons, this was a shock to the company. They thought they were good at safety and had a culture that would sustain these results. The company's president engaged me to assess the safety strategy and culture across the company. The first intervention was to join him at this location as he led a supervisor stand-down and flew in other location managers. The injured party was still in the hospital during this event.

I sat as he addressed the audience of supervisors. The managers sat along the wall to the left, where the president began admonishing the seated crowd. "Don't you know what you are supposed to do? Don't you know what you aren't supposed to do with safety?" he gruffly inquired.

Perhaps with a little more perceived political capital, an older supervisor stood up and responded, "Respectfully, sir, I don't believe that has been made clear to us." The president looked to the row of managers and questioned, "Is that true?" I watched several managers raise their shoulders to indicate they didn't know. The brave supervisor followed, "Well again, respectfully, if you all don't know, how are we supposed to?" This initiated a meaningful conversation. If you don't have everyone on the same page, this is precisely where you need to start.

In my work developing leaders in client organizations, regardless of country, industry, or type of business, I regularly find that the most critical person to shape performance and culture is the first-line supervisor. Yet, these individuals are often the most undertrained, under-resourced, and underutilized leaders in the company. Far too many super employees become supervisors—and some eventually senior executives—without being developed into the type of leaders the organization requires to succeed.

I wrote this book based on my direct observations to share tactics I have used with other leaders throughout my career. I wish you great success in your journey to becoming the best leader you can be. Don't wait on your company to invest in you. Invest in yourself and invest in those you lead. People need you, and how you show up for them makes all the difference.

Shawn M. Galloway

November 2022

# CHAPTER ONE
## *The Bare-Knuckle Bunch*

"I am the luckiest monkey in the world!"

That's what my father always said and encouraged me to believe. And why wouldn't I believe it? We lived deep in a lush, green jungle with trees that stretched farther than the eye could see, even if you were standing on top of the tallest of them. And that's what we'd do: we'd perch atop the tallest trees on the tiniest of branches, picking rare and highly desired fruits and leaves that we carried down to the ground to be packed and sold to the other animals.

As far back as anyone could remember—my father, his father, his father, and his father—we were picker monkeys, "standing in the sky," as my father put it, "to serve everyone in the jungle." I, Lucy, his eldest daughter, was part of the new generation of females to advance beyond packer monkey or sweeper monkey, ascending to the treetops as a picker monkey. I loved it!

Yes, it was dangerous. We might be bitten by snakes or spiders, and monkeys accidentally fell from the trees every day. We were usually able to catch ourselves a couple of branches down, escaping with just a bruise or two. "Tail tug" was a more serious problem. This happened when we fell through several branches, flailing with our tails to grab hold of something, finally snagging a branch but stopping so suddenly it really hurt! Then there were the "farther falls," as we called them, that could leave us with a broken bone or two, and the really serious falls, which we didn't like to think about.

  We embraced the risks, for we were the tree-top monks who went where no others dared in order to serve everyone in the jungle. Aaron and I—we'd been best friends since we were toddlers and went through picker training together—competed to see who could pick the most, climb the highest, and stand on the shakiest branch.

We weren't the most profitable of troops for, to tell the truth, we were a little too macho for our own good. Our CEO, "the Boss," as we called him, was really good about making sure the sweeper monkeys constantly patrolled the branches, sweeping away snakes, spiders, and other hazards. He was also good about giving the repair teams plenty of time and resources to shore up broken branches, pull away or patch up loose bark, and otherwise keep the trees structurally safe.

But we weren't as good as we could have been with our safety. We were a bare-knuckle bunch: "chest pounders" was what the other monkey troops called us. There was no tree too high for us to climb. There was no branch we wouldn't stand on, no matter how fragile, and we never gave much thought to harnesses and helmets, gloves, and the rest of the personal protective equipment. We knew we should have, and management hung posters reminding us to do so. But it just wasn't us!

We prized our autonomy as much as we scorned safety equipment. Our corporate structure was loose and our hierarchy pretty flat. Anyone could swing over and talk with the Boss because he spent half the day up in the treetops with us, encouraging us by his example. He knew many of us by name and would often ask about our family members.

Work was challenging for everyone, not just pickers who raced up and down the trees all day. The sweeper monkeys were constantly leaping from branch to branch and tree to tree, broom and brushes at the ready, keeping us safe. And the packer monkeys below competed to see who could pack the most boxes of fruits and leaves the fastest and with the least product damage. Sure, they could have slowed down a bit and damaged less product, but they were just as competitive as we pickers and wanted every day to be a challenge!

Our troop of chest pounders sailed along for years. Then business conditions in the jungle changed drastically. Individual troops of monkeys could no longer survive as independent operators and were forced to consolidate. Even my troop, with our reputation for daring and high-quality products, was swept into the latest round of mergers and acquisitions. We were bought by a large organization called Plant-Based Premium Bites, or PBPB for short. Our CEO was given his swinging papers. We became just another troop at PBPB, operating as part of "North Jungle Division," and were moved to an entirely different grove of trees.

Things started off all right, and we were excited to be working in a brand-new grove—a big one, with plenty of tall trees and enough precarious perches to keep our adrenalin racing. We quickly adapted, with nary a change in our routine. In fact, the only difference was that our injuries were slightly down because, this being a never-before-picked grove, the branches and bark had not been damaged. And because the packing area was set up a bit to the side, falling branches, or monkeys, were less of a hazard to the packers. Our troop was more secure than ever, as our improved injury and productivity rates demonstrated.

# CHAPTER TWO
## *Culture Clash!*

This all changed on "the day," a day we all remember. It was strange from the moment we arrived and noticed the big locker that had been set up at the edge of our grove. It was stuffed full with brand new harnesses, helmets, gloves, steel-spiked boots, and other equipment we didn't recognize.

Later that same day, some monk no one had ever seen before swung into the grove, dropped to the ground and began blowing a whistle. Five minutes later, all work had stopped, and we were assembled on the ground or in the low branches, listening as our CEO introduced himself and the rest of the C-level leadership team, plus the President of North Jungle Division and some others—even someone who headed up the Safety Department, which we didn't have before. I think his name was Gil.

The ceremony was brief, just a couple of minutes. They rushed through it so fast we couldn't catch half their names. Then they left, except the guy who blew the whistle. He went around handing out forms for us to sign, acknowledging, well, no one was quite sure what we were acknowledging. The form said, "I acknowledge that I have read and understood the above policies and procedures in their entirety and agree to abide by them." We figured it had to do with the stuff sitting in the new locker, but the whistle guy didn't actually say that. He just brusquely told us all to sign the forms, which he then collected and left. We never even knew his name, so we called him "Whistle Guy" from then on. And we never felt the need to remember the new CEO's name; we just called him "Alpha."

Yes, it was disrespectful. But we were great workers! We prided ourselves on getting the job done. We'd arrive early and stay late if we had to, we'd risk snake and spider bites, we'd climb crumbly bark, we'd race up or down the trees to help each other, and we always got the job done.

That is, we always did until "the Day." After that, things began to slide.

New levels of management popped in, so you couldn't just go up to Alpha and talk to him, like we could the Boss. You had to talk to your supervisor. Then she went to her manager, then up the chain. Nobody really knew how many levels there were, although I did chat with the head of the Safety Department one day. He was puffed up with his title, but I kept pushing him and found out that he reported to North Jungle Production, which reported to North Jungle Operations, then company HR, then company legal, then the COO, and finally Alpha. So, he wasn't high up at all.

As for us, the workers, we now had more supervisors. Before the Day, there was one supervisor for each shift, watching over the pickers, packers, and sweepers. Now there was one supervisor for pickers, one for packers, and one for sweepers, three supervisors for each shift, giving a total of nine supervisors—plus a "Manager, North Jungle Production" over the nine.

Suddenly, everything was different. We picker monkeys used to stack our equipment under certain trees and just take what we needed as we began climbing at the start of each shift. And we happily shared. When I was done with a harness, I'd toss it to a monk in the next tree or leave it where I knew someone would soon need it. Now we found ourselves standing in long lines at the big locker to check out the equipment. And "Locker Lois"—that's what we called the monk who had appeared in the equipment locker the day after "the day"—seemed to think that it all belonged to her! She frowned whenever we requested something, asked us if we really needed it, and tried to get us to take less. She'd inspect each piece carefully before handing it over, marking down every dent, scratch or tear before thrusting her clipboard at us to sign it out. Later, when we'd return it, she'd carefully check it again, muttering darkly. We figured she was keeping a list of the monks who damaged the most equipment, and that one day a bunch of us would be fired.

And it wasn't just the long locker line to get the stuff at the beginning of the shift. Since we were now personally responsible for the equipment, we couldn't share it with someone else who needed it. Instead, we had to swing all the way back down to the locker, stand in line, wait while Locker Lois inspected and checked it off on her clipboard, then climb back up. All the while, we were standing in line with the monk that needed the very same piece of equipment, but also had to swing all the way down, stand in line, endure Locker Lois's baleful glance, sign out the equipment, then climb all the way back up.

Production took a nosedive because of all these changes, which made management unhappy. We knew they were unhappy because our supervisors started urging us to "pick higher, pick faster, pick stronger!" To do this, we stopped using the safety equipment altogether. Production shot up and management was happy—until they got the quarterly safety report. All those falls, spider and snake bites, and other injuries must have made them unhappy because a billboard appeared next to the locker, jammed with posters illustrating how to use the safety equipment.

There was also a poster announcing the PBPB Safety Slogan Contest, with a bunch of slogans we were supposed to vote on. There was a stack of paper, plus a bunch of pens, and you were supposed to write your favorite slogan on the paper, fold it and stuff it into a little box. The candidate slogans were:

- Safety Is Priority Number 1
- The Key to Safety Is in Your Hands
- Never Give Safety a Day Off
- Safety First!
- A Safe Monkey Is a Happy Monkey
- Our Tribe: The Reason I Work Safely
- The Root Cause of All Falls Is Carelessness

By lunch, some monks had crossed out and rewritten the slogans so they read:

- Safety Is Priority Number 1 + (6x$92^2$) x [15z(x/7)$^3$]
- The Key to Safety Is in Locker Lois's Hands
- Never Give Safety a Day Off, but Give Me Three
- Safety First, Production Firster, Profits Firstest!
- A Soused Monkey Is a Happy Monkey
- My Salary: The Reason I Work
- The Root Cause of All Falls Is Gravity

And the monks had great fun inventing entirely new slogans of their own, the rudest of which—too rude to repeat—they wrote on the paper and stuffed into the little box.

Monks grew frustrated having to waste all that time in the locker line *and* increase production. So soon enough, they began bringing homemade safety equipment into the grove, hiding it up in the trees. If we caught a glimpse of Safety Guy in the grove, we'd all start grunting, "Safety, safety, safety!" He thought we were cheering for him, but we were really warning each other to hide the homemade stuff because your pay would be docked if you were caught with it. But having to wait in the Locker Lois line meant falling behind in picking, and your pay would be docked.

What's a monk to do?

# CHAPTER THREE
## *"Do as I Say, Not as I Say"*

It wasn't just pickers who were peeved with management.

Posters appeared in the packing area urging monks to "Pack with Pride!" and "Box with the Best!" And all the packers were given buttons imprinted with these slogans to wear. This offended them greatly because they were *already* proud of their work and *already* thought they were the best. With these new slogans, it seemed as if management was telling them they were a bunch of bums.

Yes, the packers bruised more fruit and crushed more leaves than they should have. And, yes, they could be sloppy about personal safety. They worked at a long conveyor belt, under the trees, with different monks assigned to grab and pack specific fruits or leaves as they passed by. If they stayed late to finish up and their legs got tired, they would hang from a branch by their tails and pack upside-down. Doing this for a long time caused rump inflammation, but no self-respecting packer would admit to having tired legs *and* rump inflammation, so they just kept on hanging and packing.

Another problem was that the packers' conveyor belt was pretty long, and they didn't like having to go around it. The packers tried to arrange things so they didn't have to, but once in a while they'd have to "take the trek." The younger monks, especially, did not like taking the trek. Instead, they'd get a running start and slide under the gap in the belt. Or they'd get an even bigger running start and leap right over the belt, summersaulting or twisting in the air before they landed. And if they could grab a branch mid-leap and swing around it a couple of times before landing, so much the better. This was always treated as an event, and all the packers would stop, watch, and applaud. Then other young monks would get in on the fun, sliding and leaping under and over the belt. Inevitably, some old timer would start talking about how today's slides and leaps are not as artful or daring as the slides and leaps of old, and the debate would rage.

Naturally, all this sliding and leaping produced more than a few injuries, with a slider's hair sometimes getting caught on the underside of the belt and the monk being dragged several feet until someone stopped the belt, or a leaper's ankle getting twisted or wrenched. But no one gave a grunt about that! Packers would much rather wear an injury as a badge of honor than a stupid actual badge that said, "Pack with Pride."

All this came to a stop after the Day. That's when some baboon appeared, sitting in a branch by the conveyor belt, watching to make sure no one was sliding or leaping. Yes, Alpha hired an actual 'boon to be the conveyor-belt cop. He sat there under a sign that said, "Take the Trek," pen and pad in hand, ready to take names. It's one thing that Locker Lois, Whistle Guy, and some of the other new faces were from other monkey troops. But to hire a *'boon* to police us! That really made us mad because it seemed as if Alpha was saying, "None of you monks can be trusted."

Yet, even as management was telling the packers to be careful, deliberate, and safe, their supervisors were urging them to "Pack, pack, pack!" and get more done every day. I talked with one of the packer supervisors, a friend of mine, and asked how the packers could be both slower and faster, more careful and more productive, at the same time.

"I don't know," she shrugged. "The manager is always showing us supervisors the production numbers and telling us if we don't improve them, Alpha may close down North Jungle. So I have to push the packers to produce. I don't like it, but . . ."

It's not just the packers and pickers who were mad, confused, and worried. So were the sweepers. They went head-to-head with some nasty snakes and spiders. That's why they had to undergo a rigorous training program where they learned how to identify one hundred different types of snakes and spiders, recognizing, in an instant, which were highly dangerous, slightly dangerous, annoying, or skippable. They also had to know which were on the Endangered Species List and couldn't be touched. For those guys, the sweepers set out orange cones to close off the branch and protect them.

Once the sweepers learned how to identify all the different snakes and spiders, they had to master the art of sweeping them away. Some were easy, but others were pretty aggressive; they weren't going anywhere without a fight. The sweepers had to know each snake's and spider's fighting style: were they biters, spitters, squeezers?—and how to counter it. They learned how to use brooms, brushes, nooses, forked sticks, and other tools to pin a snake's head down, which is quite the complex job! And they prided themselves on being willing to go snout-to-snout with any dangerous creature to protect the pickers.

But ever since the Day, their training was cut back. And, like the pickers, they had to spend too much time in line checking out their equipment, arguing with Locker Lois over what they truly needed, and defending themselves should any of the equipment be returned damaged, or dented, or just scuffed.

To make matters worse, they now had less "tree time" because they had to conduct ground sweeps for anteaters. Anteaters haven't been seen in this part of the jungle for years! But since the Day rolled around, sweepers have had to search for anteaters at the beginning, middle, and end of each shift and then fill out a form attesting to "anteater absence." This made absolutely no sense, so I went to see the sweepers' supervisors, all three of them, to find out why. None of them had a clue, so I checked with the Manager, North Jungle Production, who also had no idea. He suggested I talk to a picker monk in South Jungle named John who had been with PBPB since before it was PBPB, back when Alpha was just getting started in the C-suite and long before we had been amalgamated in.

So on my first day off, I swung over the South Jungle, chatted with some friends, and asked them to introduce me to John. He was indeed an old-timer, and he loved talking about the way things used to be. Here's the story he told me about the anteaters.

It seems that the very day Alpha was promoted to COO, he presented the CEO with a plan to reduce injuries and costs. Back then, they only picked and packed leaves, not fruits, and Alpha had come up with the idea of laying off all the picker monkeys and replacing them with leafcutter ants. These ants are capable of swarming up the trees, biting the leaves off, and carrying them away.

"There will be fewer injuries," Alpha explained to the CEO, "because ants rarely fall. And they don't goof off like monks do. They do what the queen ant tells them to do."

The CEO bought the idea, the pickers were sent packing, and the ants came marching in.

They were good at their work, no doubt about it. But they wouldn't wear their safety helmets because the helmets squashed their antennae, which they use to talk to each other. This was a big deal because, as it turns out, they're little chatterboxes! And they wouldn't wear the steel-toed boots they were issued because the boots were made to fit carpenter ants, not leafcutters, and they hurt. Apparently, some genius on

Alpha's staff had assumed that any ant who could cut something had to be a carpenter ant.

And here's where the anteaters come in: the presence of tens of thousands of ants attracted scores of anteaters, more than anyone had ever seen in one place. That's why the sweeper monks were told to be on guard for anteaters, and that's why the Anteater Absence Attestment form was designed.

"We've been using that form ever since," sighed John, "even though the ants were fired for talking too much, and the anteaters went away."

I was puzzled. "Doesn't anyone at headquarters wonder why we're counting anteaters when there aren't any around anymore? Don't they notice that the numbers are always zero?"

Once again, John sighed. "Do you think anyone at headquarters actually looks at the Anteater Absence Attestment forms? Half the forms we send them just get stuffed into files. No one looks at them."

I went back and explained this to Manager, North Jungle Production. But he just shrugged and said, "I don't care about the forms. My bosses are going bananas over production, so that's all I care about."

# CHAPTER FOUR
## *The Clueless Supervisor*

Another big problem arose after the Day. Personnel was shuffled around in order to staff some new groves, and they made *me* a supervisor! My title was Supervisor, North Jungle Pickers. I was delighted and loved pinning on my supervisor's badge every morning. But soon enough, I realized I knew nothing about supervising. I was a great worker, but being a great worker didn't prepare me for being a supervisor. And management didn't prepare me, either. Their attitude was, "Here's your badge. Here's your clipboard. Go to it!"

I quickly discovered that "go to it" included making sure my pickers showed up for the training sessions that management had started running. Alpha and his leadership team had gotten really worried because PBPB, which was growing rapidly, was struggling both with safety and profitability. This was very troubling, for we were operating in a competitive jungle where other animals would happily eat our lunch.

So Alpha hired a noted safety consultant who had done a great deal of work with beehives. The consultant carefully studied our operation and then made a presentation to Alpha and his leadership team. He urged Alpha to adopt a very rigid, command-and-control style of leadership. Everyone must be assigned to and trained for certain, very limited, well-defined tasks, with safety procedures built into them. Absolutely no deviation should be allowed.

"I call this the Queen/Team Strategy," the consultant explained. "Everyone is told exactly what to do and must perform exactly as specified under the control of a very strong leader." He insisted that it's very safe and effective: "Honey production is up 27 percent on average."

Alpha, who loves being bossy, announced that PBPB would instantly adopt the Queen/Team Strategy. He was quite enthusiastic about it, personally climbing the trees to scold monkeys who deviated from the program. Pretty soon, we had new safety posters featuring bees wearing our monkey safety equipment. Signs were nailed to the trees saying things such as, "Bee Safe!" and, "The Busy Bee is the Injured Bee—Take Your Time," and, "If You See a Hazard, Sting It!" I was given jars of fancy honey to award to workers "who enthusiastically embodied Queen/Team," although I was never told what enthusiastic embodiment looked like. There was also a new metric called "Sting a Hazard." Every time workers saw a hazard, they were supposed to fill out Form 975-Hazard Stung Report. The supervisor who turned in the most Hazard Stung Reports would be rewarded.

Naturally, the Queen/Team strategy was a total failure. That's because we monks, especially the pickers, are not drones. We're used to having some autonomy on the job. We're up there alone in the treetops. We have to decide if we will leap onto that shaky branch to pick some leaves, or if we will avoid other branches because the sweeper teams hadn't checked them in a while. And until Queen/Team was implemented, we decided if certain fruits were too blemished to be worth carrying down to the packers. We really resented being told to carry down every piece of fruit, then finding out that half of it had to be discarded and sold at a deep discount to the leopards who use it for their line of "Change of Spots" jelly and jam.

The good part was that we had fun making fun of Queen/Team. Quite a few of the monks showed up the day after the Queen/Team training session wearing yellow-and-black striped shirts and with stingers attached to their rumps. They referred to our grove as "the hive," and my pickers addressed me as "Queen Bee of the North." My buddy Aaron even gave me a pin showing a bee wearing a crown to wear at work.

Queen/Team certainly reduced injuries, but it also pushed down production. So after about a month, it was all over. The Queen/Team signs and posters were taken down and I was told to turn over any unused honey to Locker Lois.

Meanwhile, I was struggling with being a supervisor. All my pickers knew me as well as my whole family. They loved my can-pick attitude, so they supported me right from the start. But it was hard to tell an older monk, a friend of Dad's, that he had to wear his helmet or he wasn't meeting his production quota. I couldn't just order him around! One time I tried to get stern with a worker, telling a picker who used to babysit me and change my diapers that I'd report her refusal to follow the safety rules to the manager. She just laughed and said she'd report *me* to my mother!

Since my promotion, I had made several requests to get supervisor training. I really wanted someone to coach me and help me become a great supervisor. Finally, I was told to show up at headquarters at a certain time to take a special supervisor's seminar. I showed up early to meet my peers from the other jungles, which was great, but the seminar itself was a bust. It consisted entirely of a bored monk running through the corporate organizational chart, making it clear that we absolutely had to follow the chain of command, reading lengthy bios of Alpha and the rest of the C-suiters, and rattling off the names of the eighty-six forms we supervisors were expected to use, such as Form 569b-Quarterly Leaf Damage Assessment.

Finally, I raised my hand and asked, "Are you going to coach us on how to be good supervisors?"

Bored Monk seemed perplexed. "What do you mean?" he replied.

I put it into question form: "How do I actually supervise someone?"

He sighed and said wearily, "*Your* job is to make your pickers do *their* job. You tell them what to do; then you monitor them. If they do what you've told them to do, fill out Form 352b-Employee Compliance Report and send it on up. If they don't do what you've told them to do, fill out Form 352a-Employee Non-Compliance Report and send it on up. If you have more than ten Form 352a-Employee Non-Compliance Reports, bundle them into a Form 64d-Bundle Report, Employee Non-Compliance, and send it on up."

"What if I have more than ten excellent employees to report on? What form do I use?"

"We do not have a form for a function that has never occurred. However, in the unlikely event that ten or more employees demonstrate compliance excellence, use Form 64m-Bundle Report, Miscellaneous Multiple Employee Activity Report."

"But how do I actually supervise them? How do I make them better workers? Happier workers? Better monks?"

Again, Bored Monk sighed. "*Your* job is to make your pickers do *their* job. You tell them what to do; then you monitor them. Use the forms accordingly. And don't forget form 187z-Request for Supplemental Training."

"Training for supervisors to supervise?" I asked.

"Training for pickers to pick," he answered.

I left, armed with reams of forms but thinking the seminar was a total waste of time. I needed someone to coach me on how to be a good supervisor. A great supervisor, like the Boss. But he was long gone.

And now, Aaron was gone, too. He got fed up with Locker Lois, the anteater sweeps, and the rest of the PBPB nonsense. And when I told him what had happened at supervisor's training, with all the forms, he decided to get out of picking. He always liked technology, so he put in for a transfer to the tech staff at headquarters and was accepted.

"It'll be great," he said. "I hate standing in line, I hate stupid rules, and I love fiddling with new gadgets. "Plus," he said kiddingly, "now you've got a spy at headquarters."

# CHAPTER FIVE
## *Search for a Coach*

On my next day off, I went to visit the Boss, but it turned out he was on an extended vacation with his wife. His sister, who was tree-sitting for the couple, told me that when the Boss was feeling lost, he liked to chat with his friend Solomon the Elephant.

That name sounded vaguely familiar, so I asked who he was. She explained that he was a trusted advisor to many of the top leaders in the jungle, an expert at guiding leadership and creating cultures of extreme engagement and ownership. I didn't know what that meant, but if the Boss trusted Solomon the Elephant, I trusted him. The sister gave me directions to where Solophant—she explained that's what everyone called Solomon the Elephant—hung out, and I swung off.

Solophant lived a long way off, and it took me a long time to get there. Fortunately, the Boss's sister gave me good directions and, equally fortunately, Solophant agreed to chat with me. When I told him I wanted to learn how to become a great supervisor, he said he would help me out.

"I will serve as your coach," he said. "I will assist you in learning how to be a superior supervisor. You have spoken a lot about safety because that is what PBPB is emphasizing. But what you will learn goes beyond safety. That is because the tools used to improve safety are the same tools to improve quality, customer service, and other items."

"How can that be?" I asked. "Isn't safety, safety; quality, quality; and customer service, customer service?"

"Yes," Solophant replied, "in the sense that a tree-climbing harness, for example, is specific to safety. But not in the sense that 99 percent of the time, when an organization is struggling with safety, it is also struggling with quality, on-time performance, customer service, and most everything else. Safety is a great indicator of leadership capability. If leadership is not good at something as important as safety, you can be certain they are struggling in other areas, as well."

I scratched my head over this.

"Imagine a work area with scrap littering the floor," Solophant continued. "Animals can slip on the scrap and get injured, so you might think this is strictly a safety issue. But why is that scrap all over the floor in the first place? This is a production issue, a quality-control issue, and, ultimately, a leadership issue. Having someone sweeping the floor takes care of the scrap from a safety point of view but not from production, quality-control, or leadership points of view."

He continued. "Many leaders believe that what happens in safety stays in safety. They act as if safety exists in a bubble as a separate entity. That is a very limited way to think. Instead, you should think of safety as a window into management's mind and capabilities."

Solophant and I chatted for quite some time. I understood his point that safety is much more than an absence of injury and that the tools used to improve safety can be used to improve just about everything else in the organization. I was also eager to begin learning how to be a great leader by learning about the four areas Solophant said I had to master. They were:

- **Familiarize**—In other words, know your monkeys and what motivates them and what leadership style and skills to deploy. But there is no "best" leadership style; how you lead is situational. You need to know where you are and what you are trying to accomplish; you need to know your monkeys and what is important to them; and you

need to develop respect and trust, so you can move the collective towards the goals.
- **Focus**—There are a lot of hazards, risks, and competing priorities in any business or culture. What single thing, if concentrated on, would make the biggest difference in improving both performance and overall culture?
- **Feedback**—You don't give feedback to change what has already happened. Instead, you give it to encourage effective performance in the future. All feedback must be timely and consistent. And it must be balanced, so monkeys know how the bosses will respond if future performance is desirable and how they will respond it if is undesirable.
- **Facilitation**—Animals do things for a reason, which means that behavior, like company culture, is a byproduct. It's a byproduct of the individual choices workers make, of their superiors' behavior, and of the systems they work within. You don't change undesirable behavior by naming, blaming, shaming, or retraining. You change it by understanding why the undesirable behavior is happening, by figuring out what is making it difficult or impossible for the monks to perform as expected. Once you understand the why of behavior, you can improve the systems that animals work within. If the monks are able to perform the task as expected, the bosses should figure out how to make this repeatable. In other words, how to make it easy for the monks to perform properly. That's what facilitation means: making it easy.

Solophant thought it was a good idea to begin trying out the new leadership approach with safety. For one thing, protecting the workers is the right thing to do. It's also easier to get agreement on what needs to be done, especially when the troop is part of the solution and has ownership of the efforts. And, he added, when you see how well this new approach to leadership works in safety, you will start to see ways to use the same leadership approach in other areas. That's because when you change a company culture from "have-to" to "want-to," it's much easier to become excellent in every way.

"We could talk about these four areas forever," Solophant said. "But it is rather late already. Let's continue again sometime soon." I left, promising to return as soon as possible to begin learning about the four areas.

I was excited but realized that, as a supervisor, I had no power to put what I would learn into practice. As Bored Monk had made clear, my job was to get the pickers to do their job, apparently by filling out forms all day long and making sure the pickers sat through the latest onsites and offsites.

Meanwhile, management wasn't making my job any easier, because Queen/Team was followed by a parade of other silly safety initiatives, including "Follower-to-Leader-to-Follower," or "FTLTL" for short. FTLTL was cooked up by Alpha's leadership team, which got all excited by the latest research on birds. The Leadership Team explained to the CEO how individual birds take up the leading position at a moment's notice, suddenly turning the flock in a different direction, speeding it up or slowing it down, and so on. Then, after a while, a new leader spontaneously pops into place while the old leader becomes a follower once more. "Birds fly very high in the sky," the team explained, "often with treacherous wind currents. But their safety record is excellent because of FTLTF."

Their presentation was filled with impressive stats and diagrams of bird flocks in flight. But Alpha, who believes in strong, top-down leadership, was dead-set against the program. However, the latest injury report had frightened the Leadership Team, and they convinced him that something must be done. Alpha reluctantly signed on to FTLTF then immediately washed his hands of the program, leaving it entirely to his underlings to implement.

The Leadership Team did a splashy rollout, even giving all the monkeys badges to wear that said "FTLTF." But FTLTF flopped, largely because few monks would step up to be a leader, even for a moment. Most didn't want to stick their necks out when it was perfectly clear that Alpha was not behind this. When a few brave monkeys did step up to lead, they were quickly booted back into place by their supervisors. "Don't be an idiot," they said. "This will go away soon enough."

But we did enjoy mocking FTLTF, which we jokingly said really means "fat tomatoes, lunch-time fun."

And my monks enjoyed kidding me when they learned that I was promoted to Manager, South Jungle Production. Despite the fact that I was the most junior of supervisors in North Jungle, management was impressed by my inquisitive nature, my popularity among the monkeys, and my "outreach," as they called it, to other jungles. So, when the South Jungle Production Manager was transferred to some other facility, I was given the job. During my remaining time in North, my monks addressed me as "Lucy, Empress of the North and South." And on my last day, they threw me a farewell party during which Aaron, in from headquarters for the party, presented me with the group's parting gift. It was a crown inscribed with the words, "Please work safely today; my bonus depends on it!"

## CHAPTER SIX
## *There's More to Safety Than Safety*

I was thrilled to be promoted to Manager, South Jungle Production! I was also terrified because I still didn't know how to supervise, let alone manage, monks. And I knew that South Jungle was problematic.

Its safety numbers were decent for PBPB, with South beating North on metrics such as Sting a Hazard from "Queen/Team." But its production figures were low, and they refused to budge. Some friends in North Jungle had advised me to decline the promotion, saying that South was "like a prison." But I just couldn't pass up the opportunity.

"It's a challenge!" I kept telling myself as I swung in that first day.

"It's a disaster!" I couldn't stop telling myself after a few weeks there.

North Jungle had been loud, busy, raucous, and even rude. South Jungle was silent, still, and polite—so very polite. I was always addressed as "Manager Lucy," and when I was in the trees, branches were held steady for me as a sign of respect. The day I arrived, all the South Jungle supervisors came to greet me, praise me, and promise to assist me to the best of their abilities. But beneath the silence and sycophancy were festering feelings of anxiety and dread.

You could see this in the South monks' reaction to the squad of "Reminder Monks" who wore silver sashes across their chests and clutched thick "nasty notice pads" in their hands. The 'Minders checked to see that each monkey was wearing all the required safety gear. Monks lined up early, before the start of the shift, to get and get into their gear. And they had to be suited up and checked by starting time. One of the picker supervisors, who always looked really angry, would stand over the 'Minders as they did their checks. I called her "Furious Face."

South had also added some safety steps of its own. The 'Minders made sure picker and sweeper monks stood within the designated "jump zones" before leaping onto a tree with the zones marked by white lines painted on the ground around each tree. They also made sure that upon descending from a tree, each monk stepped into the designated "landing zone" marked on the ground in red paint. And to ensure the monks *stepped* rather than *leapt* off a tree, a horizontal blue "drop line" was painted around the base of each tree at a specified distance from the ground. The monks had to descend to this line (if not lower) before stepping off. There were many more safety lines and zones painted throughout South on the ground, in the trees, at the conveyor belt, and at the equipment locker. Should any monk stick even one toe over the line or deviate from all kinds of other rules, the 'Minders would appear instantly, rip off the appropriate notice from his pad—"Warning," "Fine," or "Retraining Required"—and hand it to the offender.

So the South monks dutifully, if sullenly, wore all the required safety equipment and stood behind all the designated lines. But despite this emphasis on safety procedures, South monks still suffered plenty of injuries. I thought I'd talk to the monks about this to get their opinions on safety. But they were reluctant to open up and mostly just said that everything was fine. On the rare occasions that they pointed to a problem, it was always something out of South's control, like the maintenance or overhaul schedules set up by headquarters.

Once in a while it seemed as if a monkey was about to come and speak to me, but then she'd stop and hurry away when she saw a supervisor. If I asked the supervisor to find that monk and bring her back to speak with me, the supe would agree to do so but never managed to return with the monk. I had this odd feeling that Furious Face or one of the other supes were somehow always hovering around, ready to swoop in should a monk approach me.

One day, I stealthily made my way up into the trees and silently observed the pickers and sweepers. I could see that they wore all the required equipment, and properly so, even though it made them clumsy and slow. But once they reached their picking or sweeping spots, they had to remove some of the equipment and set it aside in order to work. They were constantly putting the ladder on and off their backs. Their bulky helmets got in their way when they had to poke their heads into tight foliage, so they took them off. And they had to remove any equipment strapped to their belts before hanging upside down to pick or sweep. All of this maneuvering took place in tight spots, and that's where they were most likely to slip or drop something on a monk below.

Then, there were times when it was not just inconvenient but actually a bad idea to use the equipment exactly as prescribed. Sometimes putting a stepladder onto a branch to climb up and reach something on a tiny, otherwise inaccessible branch, was very useful. But if the supporting branch had a big crook or knot in it, using the ladder could make things *more* dangerous, not less. Other times, using the harness was a great safety measure. But not if some slimy creature had made the supporting branch as slippery as a greased gecko.

Common sense should have told the monks what to do, but they used the safety equipment exactly as described in the thick manuals they received when they began working in South. No matter what.

Those manuals themselves were part of the problem. They were stuffed full of instructions, way too many for any monk to memorize, so many pickers and sweepers lugged them up into the trees and often read them while walking along a branch—or even when leaping from branch to branch! Naturally, this led to a big increase in falls, tail tug, and farther falls. This became so common, monks started writing "Leapt while reading manual saying you shouldn't leap while reading" as the incident cause on the accident report sheet.

Another problem was the maintenance monks who came from headquarters and were a pretty sloppy bunch. They often left tools behind. If the monks could see the tools, they could avoid them. But if the tools were hidden under a big leaf or a bunch of foliage, they were invisible, and more than a few of my monks stepped on them and tumbled. They also got knocked on the head when tools the maintenance monks had left on a higher branch suddenly fell.

Yet another big problem was rushing to keep up with the production targets, which a lot of monkeys did. They were caught between dueling dictates: work faster *and* work safer.

It suddenly hit me: you could wear every bit of the required safety equipment, follow every single rule and procedure, and still get injured.

Solophant was right: there was more to safety than safety!

# CHAPTER SEVEN
## *Who's in Charge of This Jungle?*

I brought up all these rules, the 'Minders, and notices with my supervisors at a meeting I called. Well, I had to call the meeting several times before it happened because they kept not showing up, offering excuses that ranged from plausible to laughable:

- I overslept.
- I had the wrong date.
- I heard a monsoon was coming and was busy preparing.
- I thought this was the day Alpha was visiting and was busy tidying up the grove.
- I was busy repainting the lines for the jump and landing zones (which was not their job).
- I was busy mending rips in the 'Minder Monks' sashes (also not their job).

My favorite of all the excuses was offered by Furious Face, who said she'd lost track of time while following up on a reported sighting of an anteater. Of course, no anteaters have been seen around here for years!

When I was finally able to get them all together to present my ideas, they praised my "keen powers of observation" and "inspiring desire for improvement," then kept insisting that South Jungle had to keep all the rules because, well, because.

"South Jungle is different than North," said Furious Face.

"Yes," agreed another. "Our trees are different."

"That's not correct," I replied. "North and South have the exact same thirteen kinds of trees, mixed together, producing the exact same fruits and leaves. We receive the exact same amount of rain, and both median and mode tree height, as well as branch length and branch moisture factor, are exactly the same in North and South."

"I'm impressed by your command of the facts," said a third supe. "But the sunlight here is more diffuse, which makes our trees grow differently than North's trees."

"More acute angles in some branches," Furious Face assured me, "more obtuse in others. And the branch knot-to-crook ratio is 1.2 percent greater in South."

Yet another piped up: "Certain fruits here cling more tightly to the trees."

"And the tightly clinging fruits are more delicate, requiring more careful handling," said a fifth.

"Because of differences in wind, bringing in moisture not accounted for in the rainfall figures, the leaves here are a little larger, giving the spiders more hiding places," said Furious Face, followed immediately by yet another supe who said, "And our snakes are more aggressive."

I had no time to dwell on that possibility, for they continued to bombard me with nonsensical reasons why South Jungle was so different than North, and I gave up. I really had no idea how to manage these supervisors or to sell them on my ideas. Or if not my specific ideas, at least my attitude about how our real job was to serve everyone in the jungle by making sure our monks could do their jobs.

I didn't know how to persuade them, and I couldn't fire them or give them Retraining Required forms, so I was stuck.

But by now, I knew why South was such a mess. First of all, it was a cobbled-together jungle. As PBPB grew, it usually kept together the monkey troops it absorbed. But when they opened South Jungle they did the opposite, throwing in monks from all over the jungle. They kept transferring monks in and out of South, using it as dumping ground for those who didn't work out elsewhere. And should any monks excel in South, they were transferred to another jungle.

This meant South monks had no chance to work together long enough to get to know and trust each other. And they certainly didn't trust management, which they saw as the enemy. They whispered rumors to each other, rumors of how Alpha was spying on South Jungle by hiring detective chameleons who blended in with the leaves and listened to everything that was said; rumors of how Alpha hired hummingbirds to flit in and out of the trees, keeping an eye on the monks; rumors of how some hidden device in the helmets was recording the monks' movements through the trees; rumors on rumors:

- New research shows that plant-based diets are bad for you, so PBPB is going to close.
- Alpha is going to be fired because he let slip some embarrassing personal information in an interview.
- A few okapis got sick on South Jungle leaves and there is going to be a big recall.
- We are all going to be replaced by giraffes. This made no sense at all because giraffes don't even live in the jungle!

The only ones who felt comfortable in South were the supervisors who treated the jungle like their personal fiefdom. Right from the start—led by Furious Face, the most senior of the South supes—they bullied the pickers, packers, and sweepers, telling them that they, the supervisors, were the only bosses who mattered.

"The average manager only lasts a couple of years," they told the workers. "But we will be here for your entire career. And we're the ones who tell upper management what's going on here. If we feel you fit in, upper management feels you fit in."

They didn't have to add, "So you better do what we tell you, or else." That was well understood.

Although the supes ruled the South, they decided that they needed to excel at something to ensure their job security. They chose safety. With the help of a cooperative South Jungle Manager, several managers back, they devised new rules for South, painted the lines, set up the 'Minder Monks, and pushed for safety, safety, safety. It paid off in the sense that South won several awards for hitting safety metrics and the supes were given bonuses and awards.

Alpha praised South Jungle for winning safety metric contests and personally handed out the awards, but he was also unhappy about South's low production numbers. Lower production meant lower profits, so Alpha and his team began throwing one production initiative after another at South.

First there was this ridiculous "Hamster Cheeks" idea, which required the pickers to wear a special helmet that had two cages attached to it, one hanging down by the right cheek and the other by the left. The monks were supposed to put the fruit and leaves into these cheek cages. But the helmets were already too cumbersome without adding cheek cages!

Then there was "Fill Your Pouch," an idea brought to us by a consultant who had made his reputation working with kangaroos. Each of the South pickers was given a large pouch, worn around the neck so it was hanging down in front, to put the picked fruit and leaves in. The idea was that this would allow them to pick a lot more before heading down to Packing. The idea was sound, but the pouches were poorly cushioned, causing the fruit and leaves to be damaged. And the pouches were unwieldy, especially because they had to be worn on top of all the safety equipment. This really slowed the pickers down.

There were also incentivizing initiatives, such as "Shift Forward," which would give weekly massages for a month to the shift with the best production numbers, and "Meals by Manager," which would have the jungle's manager cook and serve lunch to the shifts that hit certain yields.

I had to sit in on meetings at headquarters where these initiatives were discussed, discarded, or finalized. I then served on the rollout teams but wasn't allowed any input, and these initiatives never jibed with the conditions in the trees in South.

The only one that even had a chance of working in our area was "Zigzag," designed to save the pickers from having to go down and up the trees so many times a day. Instead, they were to collect what they normally collected, then go to a Zigzag Station up in the trees and place what they picked in a bucket. The bucket would then be hung on ropes that went from one tree to another in a zigzag pattern, working their way down to the ground. Like a series of zip lines.

It was a good idea. The buckets were well designed to protect the fruit and leaves, and the ropes were sturdy and strategically placed. But when the buckets went from one tree to the next, they had to be transferred to the next rope. Unfortunately, the hooking/grappling/whatever-it-was device that was supposed to do the transferring didn't work well. Buckets would tip, causing fruit and leaves to fall, and buckets would knock into each other, causing them to break and the contents to fall out. It got so bad that management started tracking this with a "ZZ Droppage Rate" metric. And the 'Minder Monks on the ground had to make sure no one stood or walked under the Zigzag lines, for they might be hit on the head. They marked the danger zone with painted yellow lines and handed out Warning, Fine, and Retraining Required notices to those who crossed the yellow lines.

I went around all over South encouraging the monkeys to come up with suggestions for improving the Zigzag lines. In North Jungle the monks would have come up with all kinds of ideas, some of which were actually serious and might work. But in South, I got nothing but silence. A kind of sullen silence, as if I was endangering them by asking for input. My supervisors were even less helpful. They promised to support me in every way but came up with all kinds of excuses whenever I called meetings or asked someone to dig up information so I could write plans I wanted to pass up to headquarters.

In fact, the supes did everything they could to undermine me. They spread rumors that I was only here temporarily. They said I wasn't really the manager but that I was a corporate spy who didn't even work for PBPB. The craziest rumor of all was that I was actually Alpha in disguise!

Meanwhile, they continued their campaign for dominance, reminding the monks that while I was only going to be manager for a few years, they would be there forever. They told the workers I was a blabbermouth and would repeat anything they told me to the supervisors. And if any monk dared to stand up for me or come to me to report a problem, the supes would give him the crappiest job possible, like puttying-up woodpecker holes in the trees or lugging bins of rotten fruit out to the hyenas for recycling.

I was totally lost; I had no idea what to do. If I had really wanted someone to coach me to be a great supervisor, I was *desperate* to find a coach now that I was a manager.

## CHAPTER EIGHT
*Just Use It!*

As a manager, I got to meet lots of monks from headquarters. And right away I heard rumors that Alpha was furious that the safety numbers continued to be alarming. All of the safety metrics—bites, falls, tail tug, lost worker days, production stoppages due to injury—were problematic, to say the least.

Not a single monk believed that Alpha gave a gnat's hiccup for our safety. For one thing, he had cut back on sweeper teams. They used to do a big sweep before each shift, knocking spiders and snakes out of the trees and then run "sweep patrols" continuously throughout the shift. Now the sweeper teams were only sent out at the beginning of each shift. Not only did they spend less time sweeping, but they were trying to do their job while we were trying to do ours, which caused a lot of confusion. And we were continually battling the snakes and spiders that crept into the trees after the initial sweep. Alpha also cut back on the repair budget, which meant that we were forced to climb trees with crumbly bark, and leap onto branches that had more than a few cracks.

It was pretty clear upper management didn't care about our safety, but there was rumbling out in the jungle. Some of our big customers didn't like the idea of buying products from an "Injury, Inc.," which is what they called outfits that didn't protect their workers. A friend at headquarters told me that every time Alpha got another safety report he would pound the table, growling, "Why don't they just use their safety equipment? Just use it and keep our customers happy!"

That, apparently, was the genesis of the next great idea.

One day, Whistle Guy swung into South Jungle, gathered us together, and announced, "There's a new safety program. It's called," he stopped to check his clipboard, "it's called 'Just Use It, exclamation point.'"

Whistle Guy and Safety Guy, who stood by his side, handed thick notebooks to the South Jungle supervisors and me. "Your manager and supervisors have the new forms. New posters will go up this afternoon, and here to explain this is Bob from North Jungle Safety."

"It's not Bob," said Safety Guy, a little peeved. "It's Bill. My name is Bill, and I'm not *from* North Jungle Safety. I'm *head* of North Jungle Safety."

"OK," said Whistle Guy. "Here's Bill."

Bill launched into a lengthy presentation of "Just Use It!" The gist was that we were to use all of our safety equipment, all of the time. Put it all on when we arrive, keep it all on until we leave. Meanwhile, some monks from headquarters were laying out complete suits of safety equipment for pickers, packers, and sweepers. There was more of it than ever! But just looking at all the stuff made it instantly obvious that "Just Use It!" was a complete joke.

Here's what a new, full set of safety equipment for pickers consisted of:

- helmet
- heavily padded gloves
- shin and arm guards, to protect against bruises, bites, and thorns
- elbow and kneepads
- steel-clawed boots, for climbing
- harness, to be worn around the shoulders and belly
- stepladder, to be strapped to the back, for use in the treetops

- broom, to be strapped to the back, and a brush, to be attached to the belt, for sweeping spiders and snakes
- whistle, to hang around the neck, for summoning help
- snake-bite kit, to be attached to the belt, left side
- spider-bite kit, to be attached to the belt, right side
- goggles, to protect the eyes, with flip-down infrared lens to improve vision in dark areas
- camera, to be attached to the helmet, for scanning the sky for eagles who like to "buzz" monkeys
- olfactory sensor, to be attached to the helmet, to detect the odor of a certain dangerous snake
- auditory device, to be attached to belt, which emits a sound designed to drive away certain spiders
- "Tail Tug Reducer," to be worn around the buttocks and lower part of the tail

Nobody, not even Safety Guy, understood how the leather-and-canvas Tail Tug Reducer contraption was supposed to work. And nobody volunteered to put it on, drop from a tree, and see what happened. Several monks did, however, shout out nicknames for the gizmo, with "the Diaper" quicky emerging as the winner.

Safety Guy chose a few volunteers and timed them as they put on all the equipment as fast as they could. "We're establishing a 'Safety Dress Time' today for a baseline," he explained. "I'll be back every week to do another timing, and we'll track the improvement in 'Safety Dress Time' over time. That's going to be a big metric for PBPB!"

I don't know about the metric, but wearing all that stuff made it nearly impossible for a monk to climb and pick. The gloves were way too thick, so you had to keep pulling them off to pluck leaves. The steel-clawed boots could be driven into the trunk and did give you some stability, but they chewed up the tree, making things unsafe, and hurt your toes and ankles. Having both a stepladder and broom attached to your back, with a brush in your belt, was incredibly cumbersome. The heavy-duty elbow and kneepads were better suited to cave miners than pickers who needed much more flexible equipment. The helmet-top camera never worked properly and, well, you get the idea.

To make matters worse, it took way too long to get all of that equipment on and off. My supervisors started harassing the monks about the equipment. "You have to wear it all," the supes said over and over, "so we can fill out Form 81-Employee Certification of Safety Equipment Donning every day." In addition, they had a picker, packer, and sweeper practice putting their equipment on and off and then had these same monks "volunteer" for the Safety Dress Time Metric test every time Safety Guy came back.

The metric certainly improved over the weeks. But they were measuring the wrong thing! They should have been measuring how useful all that stuff was, not how fast we could put it on. They should have been looking for the link between their policies and the desired results, not just thumping themselves on the chest over some nonsensical metrics!

Production dropped, safety did not improve a bit, and within a few months "Just Use It!" went the way of "Queen/Team," "FTLTL," and all the other de-motivators management dumped on us. The only good part of "Just Use It!" was that the device for picking up the odor of that dangerous snake actually worked, so monks liked wearing it. But management was not metriking that, so broken detectors were not replaced, and they were eventually forgotten.

# CHAPTER NINE
## *A Very Frustrated "Monk of Mention"*

It was just a matter of time before something terrible happened in South Jungle.

It was *always* a matter of time in South Jungle: wasting time, scrambling to get things done on time, trying to make up time, wishing for more time. It was always about time, and there was never enough of it.

Workers stood in long lines waiting at the time clock, the equipment lockers, and the jump-off points for the trees; waiting for the Zigzag baskets to be fixed; waiting for the safety meetings to start because Safety Guy was always late. Workers wasted time waiting for training on how to use the equipment, then wasted more time standing in line to get signed-off on that training. They wasted time standing in line at the first aid station because they continued to get injured. Many of them wasted time pretending to work strictly according to the rules whenever a supervisor came by. Some of them wasted time trying to curry favor with the supervisors, others wasted time hiding from them—especially from Furious Face who never found an action she couldn't criticize.

Meanwhile, I was spending way too much time at headquarters suffering through endless meetings that seemed to lead to nothing except the next meeting. I was there so much because some of the higher-ups told me I was a "monk of mention," a candidate for advancement who needed to show her snout at headquarters as often as possible.

When back at South Jungle, I was swamped with paperwork, made worse by the fact that Alpha had outsourced the secretarial work to a troop of squirrels as a cost-cutting measure. The squirrels were diligent, but no one could figure out their filing system. They stashed stuff everywhere, and if they weren't there to retrieve it for you, you'd never find it. Since I did a lot of my paperwork after hours, I was always searching high and low for some form or file I desperately needed.

A lot of the paperwork was due to the fact that South Jungle went through a wave of retirements. A large number of old monks were being replaced by young monks and by misfit monks transferred in from other jungles. All of them needed to be trained, and we couldn't rely on institutional memory to help out. Injuries were up and it was no surprise because we had all the standard indicators for increased injuries: more young employees, more male employees, more untrained employees, a stressful environment, employees feeling extreme pressure to perform (the production target had been increased by 25 percent), and employees worried about their jobs.

New monks were rushed through training, and even though they didn't always learn what they were supposed to, the trainers signed them off as being qualified. Then they were cross-trained, with pickers learning how to be sweepers, packers learning picking, and so on, without any regard for what they were qualified or able to do. It took a special breed of monk to stare down a poisonous snake or stand on a slim, shaky branch to reach for fruit. Heck, a lot of the trainers themselves weren't qualified to do their jobs because they were new monks who were rushed through their own training and didn't have any practical experience at all. The only thing all this hurried training and cross-training really did was produce a better "utilization" metric, which made headquarters happy.

No one monitored the training, and no one seemed to notice that a bunch of retired monks had been pressed into service as Training Temps. It was total chaos, with one trainer teaching from the book, another from the tiny bit of experience she had gained in the past two weeks, and a third from years of experience doing it the old way. There was no longer any single "approved" way to perform any task; instead, there were multiple best (and often worst) practices.

Meanwhile, the supervisors doubled their efforts to dominate South, which generated more paperwork in the form of write-ups, warning notices, and complaints. Plus, there were more injury reports because the stress was literally causing monkeys to fall out of the trees. And get their tails caught in the leaf-compressing machines. And complain about dizziness and hearing loss caused by the high-pitched whine coming from that worthless eagle-cam. And strain their arms trying to hoist themselves into their harnesses rather than asking someone to pull the straps for them, as they were supposed to do. They were always rushing to get more picked!

I kept trying to communicate my values and priorities to my workers, but the supervisors seemed to censor the communication. It was my job to set the tone for South Jungle, but the supervisors turned a deaf ear to me.

With South being such a mess, I wondered why in the world I was a monk of mention. I later learned it was primarily because my paperwork was always filled out and sent in properly and promptly. This was a direct result of the "monkey hear, monkey do" phenomenon.

Like everyone else, from the newest hire to the C-suiters reporting directly to Alpha, I couldn't help but do what I heard my bosses talking about. Whatever they were talking about seized my attention, even if it was only talk, not directives or orders. My bosses jabber-jawed about the importance of paperwork, so I got mine done promptly and properly. This made them happy and even though South Jungle was underperforming, it made me a monk of mention.

I realized how much I was caught up in the "monkey hear, monkey do" phenomenon late one night when I was digging into old accident reports. Why, I asked myself, was I wasting time looking through musty old paperwork about things that happened way before my time? Because I heard that the COO had been saying he couldn't understand why monks were injured when we had so many safety rules. So, I decided to try to figure it out for him.

What I learned instead was how worthless those reports were, at least in South Jungle! When I was a picker, I had watched some friends fill out accident reports, and had written up several of them myself as a supervisor in North Jungle. We usually wrote a couple of paragraphs explaining what had happened. But as I went through years' worth of accident reports for South, I could see that they had all been blanded out, shrunken down, and stripped of helpful information.

They just said things like "tail tug" and "bruised knuckles on right hand," with no explanation of how the injury occurred, what the worker was doing right before being injured, or what the conditions at the scene were like. Just a brief, bland description of the injury. How could you learn how to prevent injuries if you didn't know how they happened, what system or systems had failed? How could upper management design appropriate safety controls or initiatives if they were relying on this non-info? And was it just South Jungle blanding everything out? Were the other jungles doing it, as well? Did leadership know about this? Were they deliberately closing their eyes?

I didn't know about that, but I did know that the lack of incident information wasn't stopping the tsunami of initiatives. The latest, called "Measure, Measure, Measure," or "MMM" for short, was about as ridiculous as the rest. MMM was for the sweepers and required them to carry a clipboard—in addition to their other equipment—and record numerous measurements.

They were told to write down the circumference of every branch before stepping on or hanging from it, to take a temperature reading to assess branch moisture, and calculate the distance to an adjacent branch of equal or better diameter and branch moisture, in case the branch they wanted to step onto proved to be weak or unsteady. "This is crazy," the sweepers said to each other. "We spend half our day measuring. And while we're measuring, the snakes and spiders slither and scamper to other branches. Then we have to chase them, which means measuring all over again!"

In just a few days, they figured out how to get around MMM. At the beginning of each shift, they put an already-filled-out form on their clipboards. They didn't bother measuring anything during the day unless a supervisor came by, and then they only pretended to measure. At the end of the shift, they wrote their names and the date on the pre-filled form and handed it to the supervisor. The supervisors competed to collect the highest number of forms, as Form Completion and Form Collection were the two metrics on which supervisors were judged for MMM. No one did anything with the forms or data, but Alpha awarded the winning South supervisor with a trophy and a paid vacation for Most Forms Completed and Collected.

I knew what was going on but just sighed. What was the point of telling Alpha that the forms were nonsense? By the time anyone noticed the forms had been faked, leadership would be onto a new initiative and MMM would be forgotten by everyone. That is, forgotten by everyone except by the sweepers who had always secretly referred to MMM as "meaningless maniacal micromanagement."

# CHAPTER TEN
## *A Treasured Visit*

Being Manager of South Jungle Production was a real pain in the rump! Luckily, Aaron's new job in the tech department at headquarters had him testing different tools and initiatives, so he was out in the field a lot. Whenever possible, he'd swing by for a visit.

This particular day, he brought with him a couple of what he called "treasures."

"The first," he said, grandly, "is the latest picture!" And he handed me a picture of himself, his wife Kristen, and their little twin toddlers, Dawn and Nadine.

"From your weekend at the seashore?" I asked, excitedly. "I wish I had been there!" I looked at the picture. "The girls are adorable, your wife is adorable, and you're adorable, too."

"I also brought you the latest joke."

"Not another 'two monks walk into a sparrow's nest' joke, I hope."

"No," Aaron assured me. "This one's actually funny. It's a new rule they're working on at headquarters." He waved a paper in the air, saying. "I swiped this. And I quote from that which I swiped: 'Pickers, when in the trees at or above the second branch level, shall be required to calculate the Jump Safety Factor before initiating a leap from one branch to another branch, should said branches be separated by a distance equal to, or greater than, 10.2 inches.'"

I interrupted, "Why 10.2 inches?"

"Hmmm," he replied, scanning the paper. "Ah, right here in the footnotes. Ten point two inches is the 'average picker monkey's stride length.'"

"Who knew?"

"It gets better," Aaron assured me. "Pickers also have to figure out if one branch is higher or lower than the other. Then, according to what it says here, and I again quote, 'Should said branches occupy the same horizontal plane, the picker is to check the Horizontal Plane Equality Attestment box on the calculation sheet. Should the said branches not be on the same horizontal plane, the picker is to enter the Branch Horizontal Misalignment number into the equation, along with the diameter measurements for each of said branches, at precisely the springing point on the leaping branch, plus or minus no more than 1.5 inches, and at precisely, or not more than 3.2 inches from, the intended contact spot on the landing branch.'"

Aaron stopped reading to say, "Who comes up with this stuff?" He continued, "And right here it says you have to add all that, plus the branch flexibility factor, wind speed, and temperature, into a formula, along with the number of hours and minutes that have passed since you first went into the tree. I guess the idea is that the longer you've been up the more tired you are and the less leap-able."

"Well," I said, "just trying to calculate all that will tire me out."

"Yeah, a picker will probably get two leaves picked in a day if he has to figure all this out. Oh, hey, I swiped something else. This," he said, waving a different sheet of paper in the air, "is a transcript of a presentation a very, very, *very*, high-priced consultant made at headquarters a few days ago. This is a gem. And I quote to you, right from the beginning of the presentation."

Aaron cleared his throat and now spoke like a commercial pitchman: "You've picked all the low hanging fruit, how are you going to move the needle? You don't need to reinvent the wheel, what you need is a paradigm shift, you need to get everyone out of the box and start blue sky thinking. If they aren't all giving 110 percent, you need to circle back, dive deep and peel the onion, really lean into this and ask the tough questions, address the elephant in the room, and help employees see the value proposition to answer the 'What's In It For Me?' question. At the end of the day, you need change agents who are all singing from the same sheet of music to take you to the next level. We need to make synergy and inclusion the new normal. So let me tell you about this program that would get employees to sustainably step up to the plate and . . ."

By now we were both laughing hysterically. "Did anybody buy this nonsense?" I asked.

"No, it's not nonsense," insisted Aaron. "It's pure genius. This guy gets paid a lot of money for saying absolutely nothing! This is a work of art."

"Yeah, a work of art in the BS Movement," I answered.

We chatted and laughed some more. Then Aaron invited me to dinner the next night and swung off.

I wished we had more time together.

# CHAPTER ELEVEN
## *A STEP Forward?*

For a long time, I had been trying to get the South Jungle workers engaged in, well, anything. Back in North Jungle we felt the grove belonged to us, and its success was our success. But here in South, no monk took ownership of anything—that is, no one except the supes, who wanted it all. I kept pushing headquarters for permission to try something new and was finally given the okay to set up a special safety team that would engage the workers in the process of improving safety. I called it "Safety Team, Employee Participation," or "STEP" for short.

The idea was to invite the best picker, packer, and sweeper monks to join the STEP team. They would go out and talk to the workers to get their unfiltered ideas about things such as:

- What should we be focusing on here in South?
- Which tasks are more likely to lead to injury?
- When do things not go according to plan?
- Which safety equipment is working and which is not?
- Which processes/procedures are helpful and which are not?
- Which safety initiatives have been helpful to you and which have not?
- Have you seen any hazards that have not been corrected?
- What are your concerns and suggestions?

I wanted to find out what the workers were thinking about safety and then actually do something to improve it. I really wanted to do something to get the workers to feel that the jungle was theirs, that they, their input, and their safety, mattered.

So I spent a good chunk of time chatting with the South monks to figure out who was willing to speak up, who had influence among the others, who had been around long enough to understand how things worked here, and who was not a supervisor. Based on their behavior to this point, I didn't want any of the supervisors on the team.

I made my selections and sent a list of ten names to headquarters. Two months passed before the list was approved, which seemed awfully long. Had headquarters changed its mind? I was excited to finally get the list back, stamped "Approved." Then I read it. Someone had crossed out all of my names and replaced them with ten completely different ones.

My friends at headquarters told me it was my very own supervisors who had been responsible for the changes. Working through their own friends on high, my supervisors used excuses like, "This monk is the best packer and should spend all her time working," and, "This monk is the only one who can repair the Zigzag lines and can't be spared" to eliminate my choices. Then they replaced them with ten *voluntolds*, monks who didn't even know they were on my STEP team until I informed them.

I scheduled a meeting with the voluntolds, which I had to reschedule several times because the supervisors came up with every excuse possible for not allowing the ten to come, from "I need her for the anteater sweep" to "Today? That meeting's *today*?"

Finally, I got my group together and introduced them to the concept of STEP. Even though they were new monks who didn't know much about South, weren't change agents, had no influence among the others, and were voluntolds rather than volunteers, they seemed eager. And they were especially pleased with the big pizza I had ordered for lunch, a monkey favorite: Bee Pizza, with a honey glaze and pollen dough.

We were busy making a list of questions the STEPers would ask the workers when, suddenly, Safety Guy swung into the meeting. I hadn't invited him but was delighted to see him. "Phil! Everyone, this is Phil from North Jungle Safety."

"It's not Phil," said Safety Guy, a little peeved. "It's Bill. My name is Bill, and I'm not *from* North Jungle Safety. I'm *head* of North Jungle Safety."

"Sorry. But I'm glad you're here."

"I don't mean to interrupt your meeting," he began.

"It's a safety meeting," I interrupted. "It's a new safety concept called STEP. That stands for Safety Team, Employee Participation," I said proudly.

He seemed unimpressed. "I didn't know that. But since you're having a safety meeting, technically, it's under my department."

"Aren't you *North* Jungle safety?"

"I am, but I handle safety for all the jungles."

"Have they moved you up to headquarters?" I was puzzled. Surely, if Safety had been made a PBPB-wide thing, I would have heard about it.

"No, I'm still heading up North Jungle safety. But we cover safety for all of PBPB."

"Oh." I was disappointed to learn that PBPB considered the Safety Department so unimportant. It was buried way down in North Jungle. "But you must have a much larger team now that you're handling all of PBPB."

"No," he replied, a bit embarrassed. "Same size. So, I don't mean to interrupt your meeting. I just heard that you ordered pizza from a vendor not on the list of vendors approved by Safety." He dumped a stack of papers on the table. "Here's a Form 444f-Waver, Ingestion of Non-Safety-Approved Outside Vendor Food, for each of you to fill out. Good luck with, um, the safety thing you're doing." With that, he swung out.

Much later, I learned why Safety Guy was so uninterested in our STEP safety program. It's because he was just a paper pusher. When it came to safety, headquarters made all the decisions. If a safety initiative wasn't created by someone way up high, it was filed and ignored. If someone asked about a safety initiative they had written up and submitted, they were told that headquarters was already working on something similar, which will be announced sometime next year. It was nice that the big bosses were thinking about safety but, as we saw time and again, they had absolutely no idea what the workers needed and no concept of how the needs varied from jungle to jungle, grove to grove. Most of the higher-ups rose through the "exec-prep program" and never actually worked on a tree—or even near a tree!

I was hoping to change that with STEP.

## CHAPTER TWELVE
### *It's Not About the Pizza!*

We continued our STEP meetings, always with pizza, and finalized our list of questions to ask the South workers. But right from the start the monkeys were reluctant to speak to the STEPers. When they did, they only talked about things corporate has done, like Alpha cutting back on Sweeper tree time and making them look for nonexistent anteaters. Most of the monks wouldn't say about anything specific about South, and certainly not about the supes—even the greenest of workers knew not to do that.

The upshot was that the STEP members were treated like spies. Rumors, probably started by the supervisors, began flying around:

- "The monks who talk first will be fired first."
- "If you talk to STEP, you'll be assigned to slime-scrubbing duty in the trees."
- "Jay talked, and he was seriously injured the next day! And Nina just disappeared!"

The workers sounded out warnings when the STEPers appeared with their clipboards so the others could quickly make themselves scarce. At first, they thumped a branch three times. Of course, we quickly caught on to that, so the workers ran through a series of warnings they would grunt out. One week it was "purple wire nuts," then "ducks on the pond," "pull up the gang plank," and "the eagle has landed." The "the eagle has landed" was unnerving because eagles and monkeys are natural enemies.

One day, a few of the more mischievous workers hired a particularly nasty-looking eagle to circle overhead, zero in on the STEPers in their yellow and green sashes, and "dive bomb" them.

Naturally, the STEPers panicked and ducked, and one fell on his rear, producing howls of laughter from the workers.

The supervisors continued to resist, trying to transfer my STEPers out of South, deliberately giving them "vital" assignments that had to be done during our scheduled meetings, and riling up the other workers. "The quotas still have to be met,"

they told the workers, "Even though your friends on the STEP team aren't doing their share. You have to make it up for them."

Then, the supes turned around and told my STEPers that they, the STEPers, would have to fill their quotas themselves, even if it meant unpaid overtime. Naturally, the STEPers rushed through their work, which caused more injuries. And sometimes, I wondered if the injuries were caused by rushing or by sabotage. Some of the ladders had suspicious marks on them, as if someone had tried to saw part way through them. And some of the harnesses given to my STEP team members were put together oddly, with lines and buckles in the wrong places.

I heard rumors that corporate Legal was unhappy because STEP might document some previously unknown hazards. Legal didn't want that because once PBPB became aware of a new hazard it had to do something about it, and Legal had a "see no evil" attitude toward such things.

The workers were as skeptical of STEP as they were suspicious, believing that even if they did speak to STEP about their concerns, nothing would change. We tried to assure them that as manager I had influence at headquarters, but they doubted it. And it didn't help that when we did manage to get something changed, no one seemed to notice. Or if they did notice, they didn't connect it back to us.

One of the things the South monks complained about was how long it took to get broken and creaky branches repaired. I wrote this up as a preliminary STEP Report and took it to headquarters. Apparently, Alpha got behind it because rather than waiting for Maintenance to put it on their schedule, he hired an independent group of frogs, known for their superior riveting technique, to make the repairs at night. I was delighted with the quick results, but the workers didn't seem to notice and didn't give STEP credit for this.

Luckily, the workers did open up to us a bit more over time, usually newer ones who hadn't been completely cowed by the supes. My STEPers reported that a lot of them were unhappy with the long lines at the equipment lockers. They also hated the fact that they had to fill out a Form 68bb-Replacement Equipment Request when new gloves and other personal safety equipment wore out. They felt they practically had to beg to get old safety equipment replaced, and the year's allotment was stingy. "We don't break it; it just wears out!" they complained to the STEPers.

I wrote up another preliminary STEP Report and took it to headquarters. And two weeks later, several Safety Equipment Vending Machines were set up in South. They dispensed gloves, goggles, and other smaller pieces of equipment that wore out frequently. Instead of filling out a form, the monks used their employee cards to get new equipment. And the replacement allotment for these items tripled!

This time, the workers saw the change and were very happy. But they still didn't seem to warm up to STEP. I guess they didn't make the connection between our program and the improvements.

We got a fair number of things accomplished over the next year but didn't get any credit for any of it. I admit, nothing was terribly dramatic, but little things do add up! Still, as far as the workers were concerned, the members of the STEP team got to slack off of their regular work, ask a bunch of annoying questions that didn't produce results, and go to a lot of meetings where they did nothing but eat pizza. They mockingly called the STEP program, "Safety Through Eating Pizza."

Perhaps we deserved this, for we were not communicating our progress or successes. We knew what STEP had accomplished, but the monkeys did not.

# CHAPTER THIRTEEN
## *Now What?*

It took a long time to work our way through the STEP interviews, write the reports, try to get headquarters to do something, and wonder why we got no credit for our efforts. I was definitely daunted. On the positive side, I learned that I could get headquarters to move on a few items. I also learned, on the negative side, that I had failed to engage the South workers and failed to get them to develop a sense of ownership in their jungle, their work, and their safety.

But I had gathered a lot of data and believed that was a good start. Not just about safety, but everything about PBPB. The stuff the South monks didn't like included:

- *Constant change*—jumping from one safety or production initiative to another, continually rewriting the rules, putting personnel on the "reassignment merry-go-round," and high employee turnover.
- *Hypocrisy*—management saying that they prize safety when they really prize production, doing things such as telling us to be safe but still produce as much as ever, and not wearing the personal protective equipment that we workers are expected to wear—as if they're some kind of super monkeys!
- *Unproductive activities*—having to stand in line forever at the safety locker, filling out forms and assessments that no one looks at or addresses, and going to silly safety meetings that drone on about the same irrelevant or untimely topics, such as the time we were covering Panther Prevention Week even though the panthers moved on seven years earlier.

- *Dishonesty*—"adjusting" safety reports, not telling them the real reason that injuries occur, and blaming the monkey when anything goes wrong.
- *Withholding information*—making it hard for workers to get ahold of reports, only giving summations that hide important details, and not telling us how we are doing or how we compare to our competitors.
- *Internal competition*—pitting one shift against another, which led monkeys to do things like sabotage cleanliness or hide ladders and other equipment so other shifts wouldn't meet their targets.
- *Lack of follow-up*—when we report a concern, suggestion, or near miss, and no one ever responds to the initiator.
- *Over-control*—when there is only one kind of personal protective equipment available, or not allowing us to modify procedures to fit our trees (for example, Form 45-PPa was written for trees picked by leafcutter ants, but we're monkeys!).
- *Ignoring input*—never involving us in changes and viewing us as the *targets* of a change. Aren't we the customers and consumers of safety efforts? Don't our voices matter? And if they don't, why should we care about what goes on?

My STEPers also asked the monks what management could do to make them happy, and what would inspire them to work harder. Here are the things they said they wanted:

- *Ownership*—allowing us to have a sense of pride in what we are doing and helping us see how what we do serves a purpose. We want to feel like we have autonomy and can make some decisions. We want to feel as if this is our jungle, our processes, our results.

- *Input*—allowing us to participate in activities or discussions about possible improvement and hearing from us concerning what would work or not work on the job. They want us to own safety, but what is there to own? They want us to buy into the next new thing, but they never allow us to weigh in on it. We don't make the decisions; we're just ordered to follow them!
- *Involvement*—letting us feel we are part of the process, asking us how to improve something rather than just asking our thoughts on what management has already decided to do.
- *Teamwork*—allowing us to work together to accomplish a goal, rather than just being told what to do, and recognizing what we do collectively.
- *Scorekeeping*—measuring what we are doing well or when we have successes, not just our failures. When the bosses are talking to us about the safety, quality, and productivity results, all we hear is, "Work harder to fail less," which doesn't make a lot of sense to us.
- *Improvement*—seeing problems recede or even vanish and witnessing the development of more of what we want.
- *Winning*—celebrating individuals and our team when we have met goals—really spotlighting success.
- *Variety*—offering us more than one way to do something, giving us choices so as to create ownership.
- *Recognition*—telling us individually, privately or publicly, when we have performed well, or telling us as a group when we have met a key target. Money is always nice, but an occasional "atta monkey" goes a long way!

Even though I felt I was better understanding my jungle, what motivated and demotivated my monks, I wasn't sure what to do with all this information. Sure, Alpha had responded quickly to a few of my reports—but he had ignored even more. I feared that I would write it all up, would detail and document everything, only to get the runaround from headquarters. I hated believing I was on to something good yet believing, just as much, that nothing would come of it!

There was one other thing the monks liked, which was Greg, a buddy of mine I brought in to fill the newly created position of Superintendent, South Jungle Production. Greg, who had been a sweeper in North Jungle, was fierce and fearless, tackling the biggest of snakes and nastiest of spiders without batting an eye. Though fierce when sweeping the trees, he had a charm that made you feel you were his best friend, even if you had just met. He made supervisor in North before I did, and always seemed to know exactly what to say. Even when he was telling you that you were doing something completely the wrong way, he made it sound very nice. Like he cared about you and wanted to help you succeed.

So, when PBPB gave me the budget to set up the position of Superintendent, I asked Greg to fill the slot. He would be under me, above the supervisors, and would function like a COO to my CEO. I told him South was different than North in a bad way, and that the supervisors would really resent him coming in from outside and being put above them. He was fine with that.

Greg came to South and was soon all over the grove, chatting with all the monks, sharing stories of harrowing adventures with the sweepers, and dispensing advice. He was so good at giving advice that the monks actually came to ask him for help.

So I said to him, "When I tell the monks what to do, they get resentful. I can see their tails twitching before I've gotten two sentences out. But they listen to you. How do you get them to accept your advice?"

He shrugged. "I just talk to them."

"Do you have certain things you say, phrases you use?"

"No," he answered. "I just talk to them."

I went round and round with Greg, trying to figure out his formula. But apparently, there was none. He was just naturally good at giving advice, while I was not. Over the next several months I tried being polite, stern, motherly, scholarly, folksy, even Alpha-ish with my monks. I tried everything but all I got was twitching tails.

I was desperate to learn how to be a great leader. So I decided to return to Solophant to pick up my "studies." But before I could, disaster struck.

# CHAPTER FOURTEEN
## *Heartbreak*

A troop of owls ran a think-tank called the Barnworks where they came up with all sorts of high-tech devices. They built a GPS-type device especially for tree workers or dwellers. It had a handheld screen that showed the tree you were in and all the trees around you. If you zoomed in, you could see individual branches on your tree and if you zoomed out, you could see hundreds of trees.

The Barnworks owls developed a version of this especially for PBPB, so pickers and sweepers could see the trees they were in, and by tapping on different icons they could get various sorts of information. Hit the scary face icon and you saw where snakes and spiders had been reported to be hiding. Hit the falling monkey icon and you saw which branches were broken or too thin for use. Hit the double-Z icon and you saw where the Zigzag stations were. There were dozens of these icons, all aimed at giving us information to make our jobs safer.

I found out about this device, which they were calling SAFETY RUUTZ, as in "routes," when Aaron was given one to try out. The owls had gotten permission from Alpha to beta test them in North Jungle, so Aaron and a few others from tech were asked to use SAFETY RUUTZ for a couple of weeks and report back on how they worked. Aaron let me try it and it was not bad. In fact, some of the icon-info was pretty good, like which branches had just been repaired and were safe to leap on. But other icon-info was useless, like eagle sightings. For one thing, the devices got the eagle-info from the helmet eagle cams, which never worked. For another, even if the eagle cams worked, eagles don't stand still. By the time the "eagle warning" icon lit up, the bird was long gone.

Anyway, Aaron was happily beta testing the device. He loved tapping the icons to get all that information, and one day, coming out of the trees at the end of a test run, he got very engrossed in the icon-info. So engrossed that he had his eyes fixed on SAFETY RUUTZ and not the branch he was on, and he walked right off the end of it.

That might have been okay because he wasn't that high up. But he happened to be right over the leaf compressor, and he fell right on the short conveyor belt that feeds the leaves into the compressor. He was stunned by the fall, didn't get up fast enough, and his entire right side was pulled in and pounded by the machine.

They tell me the scream was terrible.

By the time I saw Aaron, he was home, heavily bandaged, and confined to bed. I went to see him as much as possible and helped out by chatting with him and taking care of the twin toddlers so his wife, Kristen, could attend to him. Many other friends came by, and we all told Aaron we were looking forward to his complete recovery. But we knew he was never coming back, not to a jungle and not to headquarters.

Alpha and leadership sent a basket of fruit and HR sent a stack of forms to sign, but no one from headquarters came to visit Aaron. Instead, leadership buried itself in creating a new initiative called "Crush Guard." This came in the form of a fifty-page notebook detailing the exact way that various safety guards and kill switches were to be installed on the leaf compressor and its conveyor belt, exactly how lines were to be painted around the compressor, and precisely how the branches above the compressor were be trimmed weekly to specified lengths, depending on branch diameter and other factors. There were six new forms for every monk working in any jungle to sign, concerning everything under the sun, plus a list of progressive punishments to be doled out to any monk who deviated from the new procedures.

Crush Guard was launched exactly one week after Aaron's terrible injury. I knew it was coming and that South Jungle was scheduled to receive training on the initiative soon. But I didn't want to wait for Whistle Guy and Safety Guy to swing in and start blathering. Instead, I went to the grove, stopped work, and gathered everyone around.

"A new initiative called Crush Guard is being launched by PBPB," I announced. "We'll have training here in South in a few days. In fact, the new equipment and paperwork have already arrived. They're in the safety locker.

"I know what you think of these initiatives. I was a worker like you, a picker over in North. My father was a picker, as was his father, his father, and his father. I was born to be a picker and I still get that thrill when standing atop, looking out over it all.

"Like you, I know what it's like to fall or get my tail caught in something. Like you, I resented all the rules management came up with to protect us. And now, they're doing it again. The new initiative will require us to put a bunch of safety guards on the compressor and paint a bunch of lines around it showing where you can and cannot stand. It will require us to follow all kinds of new rules, to sign forms we don't understand, and to face some pretty heavy penalties if we break any of the new rules.

"What isn't included in all the paperwork is any mention of the reason behind Crush Guard. So here it is: It's because of the terrible accident that happened to my friend Aaron over in North. Aaron and I were born almost the same time, our families were close, and we practically grew up together. We used to swing over to the Big Red River together, carry rocks into the trees and drop them on the hippos' heads. We went to picking school together, and then we competed to see who could pick the most, climb the highest, leap the farthest. And we used to compare bruises because we took our share of falls.

"I introduced Aaron to his wife, Kristen, and I'm god-monk to their little twins, Dawn and Nadine." I held up a picture of Aaron, Kristen, and the twins as I said this, then passed it around.

"Aaron was testing a new safety device when he fell from a tree onto the compressor conveyor belt." I could see by the monk's reaction that they instantly guessed what I would say next. "The right side of his body was pulled in and, well, it was a terrible thing. He'll never work again.

"I've been sitting with Aaron and Kristen this past week. They're trying to figure out what to do and how to raise the kids now that he can't work anymore. Aaron can deal with the physical pain, but he can't stand the idea of not being a good father and provider to his little girls. And I can't stand the idea that I might have to sit with one of you and your loved ones, seeing you in pain and trying to figure out how to move ahead somehow. So please, let's follow the new rules. Let's all look out for each other, and let's all make this jungle as safe as it can be."

With that, I picked up my stuff and left. And even though my workday had just begun, I swung out of South and went to see Aaron.

# CHAPTER FIFTEEN
## *Learning to Lead by Coaching*

When I got to work the next day, I was greeted by a tall stack of papers sitting on my desk. Looking through it, I was surprised to see that every monk in South had signed the Crush Guard paperwork—all six of the forms. It usually takes several days to get about half the monks to sign and weeks to chase down the rest.

And when I went to the grove, I saw that all the guards had been installed on the compactor, all the lines painted, and all the branches trimmed. Usually, it takes weeks to figure these things out, with arguments over how to do it, calls to maintenance for help, complaints about the new stuff and adjustments to it, and a whole lot of rump-dragging. But there it was, all done, the day after I explained what had happened.

I was pleased but also depressed. Does it really take a total disaster to get something done in PBPB? And will this program actually work? If it's anything like the rest of the safety initiatives, it will be tossed aside as soon as the workers start feeling the pressure to meet their quotas, which go up but never down.

Once again, I left work early. After visiting Aaron, I sped across the jungle to see if I could talk to Solophant. I wanted to know if it was possible to

- teach workers to make safety a priority,
- get workers to follow the safety rules without feeling resentful,
- get workers *not* to follow any safety rules that were silly or actually harmful,
- get management to stop dumping all of these ridiculous rules on us, and

- get management to stop making workers choose between safety and production.

In other words, as I admitted to Solophant, I was asking for a miracle.

"Not necessarily," he said. "As you recall, one need not choose between safety and production. Properly done, the items and attitudes that improve safety will also improve production, customer service, on-time performance, and everything else. Let's return to the four areas we talked about last time: leadership style, focus, feedback, facilitation. Let's start with leadership style. What kind of leaders are there?" he asked.

"Well, Alpha likes to boss everyone around. But our old boss, before we joined PBPB, never bossed anyone around. He just gave suggestions, and we followed them because they made sense. I guess he was smarter than Alpha."

Solophant shook his head. "Not necessarily, for there is a difference between leadership smarts and leadership style. Think about the different animals. How do their leaders lead?"

"Hmmmm. Well, the ants obey their queen because, I guess, that's all they know how to do. The meerkats are organized like a cooperative. The wolves have a co-leadership approach: the top male and female lead together, and everyone else in the pack has predefined roles and responsibilities. With horses, leadership is shared, and the entire herd teaches the babies and other new members how to behave. And, of course, the lions are super command-and-control, with the top guy kicking the others around. It's all hostile takeovers with the old and the upcoming leaders fighting it out, trying to destroy each other. For the rest of the lions, it's pretty punitive. You do what the leader says, or else.

"We elephants," continued Solophant, "are on the other end of the spectrum from the lions. Our leader does not push us around. Instead, she—and it's always a she—is chosen because of her wisdom and experience. We follow her because we trust her."

We continued reviewing the leadership styles of the various animal groups and then I mentioned Greg, my superintendent. "He doesn't lead at all. He didn't even tell anyone he was Superintendent when he came to South Jungle, and he never wears his Superintendent badge. I suppose some monks still don't know his title. He never really leads, but they always follow him."

I described a few encounters between Greg and others I had observed. "Ah," said Solophant. "He is a coach. That is a powerful form of leadership under the right circumstances."

"What do you mean?"

"As to the right circumstances, suppose South Jungle catches fire. There's no time for collective leadership, with everyone offering their own opinions. And there is no time for coaching. When things are on fire, you need a strong boss making decisions and you want monkeys to obey, now!"

Solophant continued. "Always remember that leadership is situational; it depends on the particulars of the workforce, goals, capabilities, and other factors. If you are trying to get more out of monkeys, the command-and-control leadership style of a lion, or of the Queen/Team initiative, will not get you where you want to be. Neither will a bird-style, 'Follower-to-Leader-to-Follower' or a cooperative meerkat approach. It sounds as if you require exactly what you see your superintendent doing: coaching."

"Great! How do I coach?"

"You begin by identifying what you want your monkeys to do. Be sure to define it in terms of desired performance and desired outcomes, such as 'using the stepladder properly,' rather than in terms of results, such as 'not getting hurt.' You must provide feedback to your monkeys, both when they are performing and when they are not. When they are *not* performing, you need to identity why and address the reasons for their nonperformance. Think of it this way: coaching is about helping your tribe perform at their best, recognizing them when they are, and working to make it possible, as well as easier, for them when they are not."

I tried to sum coaching up: "One, figure out what performance I want from the monks. That's performance, not results. Two, give feedback all the time—feedback when they're performing, feedback when they are not. Three, if they are not performing, figure out why and help them get back on track. Right?"

"Yes, good. And good luck."

# CHAPTER SIXTEEN
## *Battling Snakes of Different Sorts*

I decided to coach my monks. But I didn't want to roll out some kind of "It's Coaching Time!" initiative or anything like that because I didn't know how my coaching would go over in South. So I thought I'd start small by making my way through the jungle every Friday, looking to speak to at least five monks in order to learn something about them. I wanted to understand better how to increase the things that motivated them and decrease the things that demotivated them. I'd also ask them if they had any concerns.

I didn't really know any of the workers, so I took Greg with me at first. When we saw a monk up ahead, he would tell me her name and something about her. I'd then approach her by myself and say something like, "Hi, Blanche. I'm Lucy, the manager. I hear you were raised in the Big Red River area. Did you ever climb up in the trees and drop rocks on the hippos' heads? I did that a lot when I was a kid."

I'd ask them how many children they had, what their favorite foods were, where they were born, how many years they'd been a picker/packer/sweeper—whatever I could think of based on Greg's info or what I'd gleaned from our conversations. A lot of times they didn't say much. They were probably shocked that a PBPB manager was actually asking them about themselves. Maybe they thought it was some kind of trick. But a modest number responded with something more than a mumble, and I managed to speak to five monks every single Friday and learn something about each one. And I'd always end the conversation by asking if they had any concerns about anything in South Jungle.

Sometimes I'd run into one whom I'd talked to earlier, and I would pick up the conversation where we'd left off last time. I remember seeing a monk who had told me his son played Little Jungle Baseball and had a big game coming up. When I saw him again the next week I said, "Wasn't your son's Little Jungle team going to play the Alligators?"

"No, the Crickets."

"The Crickets! How'd the game go?"

Over time, more and more monks began to chat with me, but very few were willing to tell me their concerns. Still, once in a while someone would say something that was a bit shocking. When I asked one monk if she had any concerns about safety, she said, "I've worked as a packer my entire career. I'm going to retire in three weeks and the only time any boss has spoken to be about safety was to criticize me and tell me I was doing wrong. For once, I wish someone would tell me what I'm doing right!"

One Friday, while touring South Jungle, I was chatting with a picker when suddenly we heard a terrible rustling in the tree above us, coupled with the sound of breaking branches that seemed to come closer and closer. We looked up and couldn't see anything, for the foliage was very thick. Then, all of a sudden, something came crashing out of the branches and slammed into the ground.

We couldn't figure out what "the thing" was as it roiled and rolled, flinging its limbs out, crashing this way and that. It took a couple seconds for us to realize it was a sweeper monk and a giant python locked in a battle to the death. We gasped with horror as the snake suddenly broke its head out of the sweeper's net and started to swallow the monk's leg whole!

In an instant, we jumped on the snake along with a bunch of nearby monks and tried to hold it down while other monks grabbed the sweeper monk and tried to pull his leg out of the snake's mouth!

With all of this thrashing, fighting, screaming, and adrenaline, it's impossible to say exactly what happened. All I know is that suddenly we monks were lying on the ground, panting in exhaustion. The sweeper monk who had been battling the python was lying there with us. But the snake was gone.

The sweeper seemed to be okay, but I told him to go get checked out and then take some time off.

It didn't take long before everyone in South heard what had happened. The sweeper, whose name was Cade, had been conducting an anteater check when he suddenly came upon the biggest python he had ever laid eyes on! Even though he didn't have his full set of equipment on, he leapt into the trees and got on the snake's tail—literally! The snake managed to get away and slither higher and higher up the tree, battling it out with Cade all the way.

"I'd never seen a snake so big or so aggressive," Cade wrote in his report. "It was like fighting three regular snakes at once."

Although he was without his whistle and could not summon help, Cade refused to give in. He and the snake were locked in mortal combat with Cade's right hand and arm in the snake's mouth and the snake's head entangled in Cade's net when they fell and crashed to the ground. The rest of the story you already know.

Horrified, I went to headquarters and asked, cajoled, reasoned with, screamed at, entreated, and threatened everyone I could, insisting that I had to have more budget to protect my sweepers. I got it and decided to set up a new position called Sweeper Spotter. My idea was that there would be a sweeper "spotter" assigned to every fifteenth tree. He would climb high then sit there, waiting, listening for any sound of danger in the trees nearby. He wouldn't be burdened down with all the sweeper gear; he would just have a swingie-talkie to communicate with other sweepers. If he saw or heard any signs of trouble, he was to call in help, but he himself would stay out of the fight.

I called my sweepers together to explain this to them, and they were not pleased. I could see it in their eyes and twitching tails, but none of them spoke up. Finally, a few of the monks I had met on my Friday chats spoke up. They said that being a Spotter and sitting in a tree all day would be boring. You can't be super-attentive all day long. They didn't like the idea that the Spotter would be "unarmed" and unable to join in the fight because sweepers are an aggressive bunch. And they didn't like the suggestion that a sweeper might even need help. "You're making us look like sissies," one of them grunted at me.

I didn't know how to respond. I thought they'd love my idea—and love me, too—but they hated it. I felt angry, insulted, and was about to say, "That's what we're going to do," and close the meeting. But then I remembered what Solophant told me.

So I said, "We pickers like to tease you sweepers, saying you spend all day doing nothing but lean on your brooms. But we really do admire you. We all have our own stories of being surprised by snakes or spiders, thinking we're in big trouble, then out of nowhere being saved by a sweeper who knew exactly how to deal with the danger. You sweepers keep us safe, and I'd like to return the favor by keeping you safe. So please, tell me how I can do that."

They seemed shocked: a manager was asking for their ideas?

"Over the next two weeks or so," I continued, "I'd like you to think about how to improve the Sweeper Spotter program. Stop me in the grove to give me your ideas, or drop by my office, or send me a note—whatever you're comfortable doing. I really want your input."

84

During the next two weeks, quite a few sweepers gave me ideas. There were ideas about how many trees a spotter would be responsible for, rotating spotters in and out, adding to their equipment, and so on. Whenever I used a suggestion, I went back to the sweeper who made it and let him know his idea was helpful and being used. I even had little coins made up with the PBPB logo that I gave to the suggesters. I called them "Coach Coins." They weren't worth anything, but the recipients seemed pleased to get them. I guess it gave them an "atta-monk" feeling every time they looked at the coin.

I launched the Sweeper Spotter program several weeks later, personally introducing it rather than relying on Whistle Guy and Safety Guy. And it was a success! I can't honestly say if the program with the sweeps' input was better than mine because we never tried mine out. But I can say that the sweepers embraced the idea, which automatically made "their" program much better than mine.

But if the sweeps loved the program, the supes definitely did not. They were furious because, as one of the sweeps quietly informed me, "By establishing relationships directly with the workers, you're breaking the supes' hold on South."

The supervisors retaliated by withholding their paperwork, which essentially meant they went on strike. They gave Greg and me one excuse after another for not producing various forms on time. And when we finally got the papers, they were improperly filled out or only half finished. When I told them to cut it out, they went the other way, hitting us with a blizzard of paperwork, including forms we had never seen before. Things like Form 65a—Misty Morning Wetness Warning, Form 158—Crocodile Hazard Assessment, Form 42—Goal Zero This Week's Hero, and even Form 174cx—Helmet and Boot-Wearing Compliance Percentage. This last form was created back when Alpha replaced the pickers with leafcutter ants. All of these forms were still on the books, so, technically, the supes were right to dump them on us. But it was ridiculous!

The supervisors also told the Reminder Monks to be extra strict in handing out notices for the slightest infraction. The supes themselves spent more time than ever in the grove, harassing the workers in an attempt to reestablish their control over the jungle. And they used their connections at headquarters to spread rumors about me. Things like I was a spy for our biggest competitor, Great Grove Goodies, or that I was really Alpha in disguise for that popular show, "Clandestine Monkey." This made absolutely no sense. Lots of monks at headquarters knew Alpha personally and could see for themselves that I wasn't him. We weren't even the same size! But that didn't stop the rumor from spreading.

Dealing with all this craziness made fighting a super snake in a tree seem like a cakewalk.

## CHAPTER SEVENTEEN
## *What Does Success Look Like?*

Despite the struggles with my snaky supervisors, I was feeling good about something—my coaching. I even made a list of my coaching accomplishments to show Solophant:

- I developed relationships directly with my workers, getting to know their names and things about their families, what they like, or what they do in their spare time.
- I got everyone to follow the "Crush Guard" initiative by personally introducing it, explaining why it was so important, and showing what's in it for them.
- I invited the sweepers to add their ideas to my Sweeper Spotter program, telling them when I used their ideas and giving Coach Coins to those who contributed ideas.
- I initiated the STEP team, collected comments from the monks, and followed up by handling some of the problems they mentioned.

I was pretty proud of my coaching and expected Solophant to trumpet his approval when I showed him the list. But all I got was a measly little ear waggle.

"It is an excellent beginning," he said when I took a personal day to swing over and chat with him. "You have learned several techniques of coaching. But remember that these are coaching techniques and tools, rather than the actual coaching."

I was puzzled. "What's the difference?"

"Ask yourself this: What am I coaching for?"

"What do you mean?"

"What does success look like to you? Imagine that you could leap ahead five years into the future and see the results of your coaching. What would that look like in South Grove? What would the results be? What common behaviors would you see across South Grove that would explain what led to an improvement in the results?"

"Well," I said, thinking hard, "all the monkeys would be following the safety rules and the other rules. The area around the conveyor belt and other machinery would be perfectly clean, the safety equipment would be used properly, and we would meet all the safety benchmarks and production quotas. We would have safety systems and controls that are dealing with the work hazards as the monks are working—successfully dealing with them."

Solophant shook his head impatiently. "You are talking about results, which you cannot coach for. What you can coach for is *behaviors*, specifically behaviors that lead to the desired results. When coaches train their athletes for the Jungle Games, they don't teach them how to win a medal. Instead, they coach for the *behaviors* that lead to superior performance. At the last Jungle Games, did you see 'Rocket' Rhino win the high jump?"

"He's phenomenal! That 'rhine can fly!"

"Yes, he can. But he did not train by practicing to receive the gold medal. Instead, his coach worked with him on the behaviors that lead to great high jumping. Behaviors such as turning the head toward the shoulder at the right moment, initiating the leap with only one foot, not four, and rotating around a vertical access."

That sounded pretty clear to me. "OK, got it! You coach for the desired behaviors, not the outcome. If monks absorb, internalize, take ownership of, and make the desired behaviors natural and automatic, you'll get the outcome you want. But how do I do that?"

"Your coaching should be organized around focus, feedback, and facilitation," said Solophant. "You begin by knowing what you are coaching for—what things will look like in the perfect future. In order to get to that perfect future, you must determine what you want your workers to focus on. Then you must encourage them with the proper feedback. Finally, you must facilitate. That is, discover what influences monks to take risks, remove roadblocks to the desired behavior, and provide a balance of consequences—consequences for performance and consequences for nonperformance—to nudge them in the right direction. That is quite a bit to tackle at once, so I recommend you begin with focus."

"OK. What do I want my workers to focus on?"

"Go back to your jungle, talk to the workers, and find out what would enable and produce the behavior that leads to the desired result. That should be the focus."

Solophant and I talked more about coaching and focus. We decided that because of the leadership trust issues, the STEP team would talk to the workers, while Greg and I went through the paperwork. Between the talking and paper digging, I would figure out what we needed to focus on.

Naturally, upon returning to South Jungle the next day, I was greeted by yet another injury. Luckily, it wasn't too serious. It happened to Machine Monk Max, an old-timer who knew better than anyone how to keep the packing conveyor belt running.

The conveyor line had a great new source of energy generated by rhinos running as fast as they could and smashing headlong into the biggest tree trunks in the grove. The trunks were wrapped with new-fangled K2E Pads that converted the kinetic energy of the rhinos' running and crashing into the electric energy that ran the packing belt. The K2E Pads were dreamed up by the Barnworks owls.

But if the energy source was high tech, the conveyor belt was not. It's the Model H, originally designed to be powered by hamsters running in wheels. So even at its best, the conveyor belt was about as reliable and energetic as a sloth on a slow day.

Machine Monk Max was the only monk who could keep the darn thing running. He stood on a branch-walk not too high in the air and ran back and forth between the conveyor belt and the trees wrapped with the K2E Pads. It was quite a distance. He spent most of his time above the conveyor belt, monitoring the control panel, turning dials to regulate flow of electricity, checking stress fracture readings for the trees the rhinos were crashing into, pouring oil into different tubes, and doing other things I can't explain. Every once in a while, he dashed to the other end of the branch-walk to pick up boxes of oil cans, stacking them high in his arms and then racing back to his station to check the readouts and pour oil into the tubes.

The problem was that the boxes of oil cans were delivered in dribbles, just one every half hour. They were put on the K2E Pad end of the branch-walk, far away from where Max monitored the machines. He didn't like to leave his station just to pick up a single box, so he waited until many boxes had been delivered, then raced across the branch-walk, grabbed a big stack of boxes, and hurried back to his station. The boxes were stacked too high in his arms for him to see what was directly ahead, but he'd been managing to run along the branch-walk essentially blind for years.

Well, the day I returned to South after talking to Solophant, a maintenance monk was working in the grove, refreshing the painted lines. He was finished with one brush and, instead of putting it into his apron pocket, he set it on the branch-walk, figuring he'd get it later. And, naturally, Machine Monk Max, his arms full of boxes, stepped on it and went flying, right off the branch-walk. His fall was cushioned because he landed on a couple of monks who were knuckling by, and, thankfully, they only suffered a few bruises between them.

It was not a spectacular accident. What was spectacular was the response to it, which I saw because I happened to be there when it happened.

The moment Max hit the ground, two 'Minder Monks appeared out of nowhere and began handing out Warning, Fine, and Retraining Required notices to everyone in sight. The packing supervisor was suddenly there, simultaneously scolding Max, the maintenance monk, and the conveyor belt crew chief for the accident. While she scolded these three for the accident that just happened, she also scolded two other monks for a similar paintbrush accident that had happened three months ago. She was chewing out five monks all at once! That was an impressive piece of multitasking but totally inappropriate.

I interrupted the supervisor, thanked her for her interest, and told her I would take it from there. Then I collected all the 'Minder Monk notices and told the monks who received them that the notices would be canceled. I sent Max and the monks he fell on top of to get checked out and asked the Maintenance Monk to fill out an accident report. Everybody got back to work and, this being a rather routine accident, it was quickly forgotten.

But not by me. I thought it would be the perfect way to start my STEP, Round Two, with a focus on focus.

## CHAPTER EIGHTEEN
### *Let's Go with the Pizza!*

I called together my STEPers and told them we were going back out to the monks to ask them how they performed various tasks, where and how they think injuries occur, what might influence them to take risks or make it difficult to perform their tasks, and so on.

This time, the South Jungle monks were more willing to talk, partially because I had already developed relationships with a number of them, and Greg had established even more. They were also starting to feel that I was on their side once I canceled all the 'Minder Monk notices after Machine Monk Max's injury.

I also turned the mockery about "safety through eating pizza" into a plus by giving out free pizza. Everyone who talked to one of my STEPers got a coupon for a free, whale-sized pizza. They could choose from

- Panther Pizza, with, as the slogan said, sauce spread by panther tail for a *"Purrrrrrfectly smooth pizza experience"*
- Zebra Pizza, *"Painted with stripes of delicious delights"*
- Python Pizza, *"So scrumptious you'll want to swallow it whole"*
- Parrot Pizza, *"So tasty, you can't stop talking about it"*
- and, of course, Bee Pizza, with pollen-dough and honey glazing.

Not only would they get a premium pizza, but it would be delivered by Chuber, a service run by the cheetahs, the fastest animals alive, to make sure it arrived piping hot.

My STEPers conducted scores of interviews, learning some very interesting things about what the South monks did and thought on the job:

- There's not enough oversight, not enough monks on the ground to give us feedback.
- We're confused because new monks are training other new monks, so there's no standardization and way too many "common practices."
- It's hard to keep track of our gloves. Sometimes we have to take them off and put them down to get something done. Then we forget them.
- We can't see that well when we pick at night because the lighting isn't good—too bright in some areas and practically nonexistent in others.
- We keep getting smacked in the face, or rump, by branches that were tied back but let loose when the ties broke.
- We know safety is important to Manager Lucy, but we're measured by how much we pick. We're always being reminded about that "pick and pack yield" but hardly ever about safety.
- There aren't enough stepstools and ladders to go around, and the good ones are always locked up in the locker. You tell us to use them, but they aren't available.

Meanwhile, Greg and I were digging through the South Jungle files looking at accident report forms. Going back years, the accident reports had been blanded out, saying nothing more than "tail tug," "bruised knuckles on right hand," or something else vague and innocuous—and totally useless. But way in the back, in unmarked boxes, we found the original accident reports, the ones actually written by the monks involved or by witness monks. Now, with actual descriptions of the incidents to study, Greg and I began to get a sense of why monkeys are injured in

South. The specifics were different for pickers, packers, and sweepers, but there were a lot of commonalities:

- There are more injuries to the hand than any other part of the monkey.
- Injuries tend to occur more often right before and after lunch, and more on Mondays than any other day of the week.
- Monks are more likely to be injured if they have less than six months of experience in the trees.
- A lot of incidents could be prevented by improving how and on what the monks are climbing or standing.
- A surprising number of injuries occur because monks are struck or injured by something making contact with them, such as getting smacked in the face by a branch or conked on the head by a falling tool.

Greg, the STEPers, and I went over and over the data, making sure we truly understood why monks were getting injured in South Jungle, what we might be able to do about it, and what couple of things we could focus on to help monks start getting safe. And this time around, I told my STEPers that we had no secrets, that it was all right to chat with other monks about what we were doing in our STEP meetings. I wanted all the monks to know that we were doing more than eating pizza, and to realize that their input was being taken seriously.

Finally, we were ready and rolled out the "I Can HELP Myself Be Safe" focus initiative. I introduced it personally and began by thanking the STEPers and all the monks for their contributions. Then I made a joke about how we've all put on a few too many pounds eating all that pizza and awarded a Coach Coin and an extra day of paid vacation to the monk who contributed the most ideas to the initiative. It was actually a tie, with two monks contributing the same number of ideas. But Greg had checked with the two winners beforehand and found out that one of them didn't like the idea of having to stand up in front of a big crowd. So I gave him his coin and extra paid vacation day privately. Then I explained the essence of the "I Can HELP Myself Be Safe" focus initiative.

"There are many types of accidents," I said, "so you might think you need special rules for each. But if you look at all the accidents, you'll see that if we focus on the few things that can help us understand how to prevent the huge majority of injuries, we can really reduce accidents. To help you remember what we need to focus on, think of HELP: H for hands, E for eyes, L for line of fire, and P for position of your feet.

"Let me explain:

- "For H, hands, think about where you're putting your hands, whether or not gloves are needed, and what kind of gloves are needed.
- "For E, eyes, think of keeping your eyes focused on the path or direction you are traveling. And don't put any part of your body in that path unless you've looked there, and your eyes have scanned the area.
- "For L, line of fire, think about something in motion coming at you. For example, if you're near a branch that's being pulled back, think about what would happen if it's released. If you're on the ground and getting close to the Zigzag lines above, think about what would happen if the lines or buckets fell. If you're cutting something, think about cutting away from yourself, not toward.
- "For P, position of your feet, think about what you are standing, walking, or climbing on. Think about the position of your footing and about having three points of contact. That might mean having two feet on the ground or branch, and one on a railing; or two feet and a tail; or

a tail, a hand, and a foot; whatever makes the most sense. Ask yourself, is what I'm standing on or climbing giving me good, solid, steady footing?"

I knew there was more to it than just focusing the monks. It wasn't only on them to prevent injuries, we bosses had to do our part, too. But I gave more examples, answered questions, and wished everyone good luck "as you start to HELP yourself be safe. I really want this to work because I'm concerned about you. I've experienced injuries firsthand, and Superintendent Greg and I have just read hundreds of accident reports going back years. I want to HELP you be safe, and the best way I can do that is to encourage you to HELP yourselves be safe. I know you can do it!"

The presentation seemed to go well, and Greg and I spent loads of time in South Jungle over the next many months, in the trees and on the ground, talking with every monk we could. We'd ask them if they remembered what HELP stood for, and if they didn't, we'd repeat the words: hands, eyes, line of fire, position of feet. Pretty soon, the monks started saying "hands, eyes, line of fire, position of feet" to me or Greg as soon as we knuckled up to them. When they did that, we'd thank them for helping to make everyone in South safer.

We'd also thank anyone we saw doing HELP behaviors like wearing the right gloves, keeping their eyes focused ahead when reaching for the next branch to swing on (instead of grabbing a snake!), or positioning their feet closer to the tree trunk before leaping to another tree for better stability.

And when we saw monks that were not taking the HELP precautions, we didn't scold them or slap them with a warning. Instead, we tried to figure out why. We expressed our concern to the monks and talked with them to learn why the precaution wasn't being taken or maybe couldn't be taken. This was important because if one monkey was influenced to take a risk by something or someone, other monks doing the same task might be influenced by the same thing. So if we figured out the reason why one monk was taking risks, we might figure out why others were doing the same.

One day, a surprising thing happened when Greg and I had just finished thanking a worker for being so HELP-ish. A South supervisor came up and asked if he could tag along and see what we were doing. This was Larry, a sweeper supervisor I had thought was sort of on my side—or, at least, not out-and-out against me. More like neutral. He tagged along with Greg and me several times over the next couple of weeks, tried coaching, and said it seemed to work. I was delighted: Larry was our first supervisor convert!

The final part of the program was to let the monks know their efforts were working, or, in other words, communicate the results to them. Otherwise, as Solophant had pointed out, there would be an excellent chance that the monks would believe their efforts were for naught and stop HELPing. Over the next several months, as reports came in, Greg and I made a point of telling the monks that their efforts were being rewarded with success. We'd show them charts with the latest figures and thank them for their help.

I was feeling good about the way things were going in South. Not only were the safety reports looking good, other indicators were also improving quite nicely. But, as I learned, the jungle is full of surprises, and just when you think things are going well, you learn they're not.

## CHAPTER NINETEEN
*No Monk Injured on My Watch!*

It was delivery day in South Jungle, and the packers were eagerly awaiting their first look at the new conveyor belt. Well, it wasn't entirely new because the underlying machinery was the same. But the belt itself was being replaced and raised several inches because walkways were going to be installed on either side of the conveyor line. The walkways had special, cushioned, nonslip surfaces that would relieve strain on the packer monks' backs and feet while reducing slips and falls and making it impossible for monks to slide under the belt. Since the new walkways were several inches above the ground, the new conveyor belt had to be raised accordingly, with the exact amount determined by an ergonomic study of monks in the process of packing. The Barnworks owls who designed it assured Alpha the new conveyor was well worth the price. I had seen models of it at headquarters, and it looked great!

The conveyor belt had been installed overnight, and I got to South early the next morning to inspect it. It was just as impressive as it had been in the models. But the monks who assembled it were not looking happy.

"What's wrong?" I asked, fearing the answer.

"I don't know," answered the shame-faced assembly crew chief. "We followed the directions, but . . ." He finished his sentence by gesturing to the machinery.

I looked closely at the packing line, watched as a few packer monks got on, and suddenly it hit me: The belt was not high enough. The packers working on the walkways had to bend over, so instead of reducing strain on the monks' backs, it would actually increase strain!

It took me a little while to figure out what had happened. When Alpha okayed the purchase, he neglected to specify that he wanted the owls to install the new machinery and walkways. Instead, some monks from headquarters did it, saving us some money. The headquarters monks followed the instructions perfectly, but they did not account for some rippling in the ground around the conveyor belt. The owl installers would have had the know-how and equipment to make adjustments on the fly, and everything would have been all right. But our monkey installers did not have the know-how and equipment. That's how we wound up with a conveyor belt that was too low relative to the walkways, which would cause *more* back pain and other problems.

I had no idea what to do! I didn't want my packers suffering more injuries but knew that the Barnworks had closed very early that day so the owls could prepare for the Hoo's-Hoo Dusk to Dawn Gala, a pretty important event on their calendar. That meant, at best, no one could fly in to fix the belt until the next day, and it could take yet another day if they had to take the whole thing apart and start from scratch.

By this time, the packer supervisor had ordered the belt turned on and packers were on the walkways, packing away. Some were bending over too far, while others were trying to adjust for the height problem by bending their knees too much. Still others were hanging from branches above, packing upside down. And we all knew what problem that would lead to!

I was so fed up that, even though I didn't have the authority to shut down the packing line, I did it. I went down the line telling monks to step back and then shouted up to Machine Monk Max to hit the emergency stop button and turn the whole thing off.

Then we all stood there, the monks looking at me, and me looking at, well, I don't remember what I was looking at. I do remember thinking I'm going to be fired, but it will be for a good cause. A *great* cause!

Soon enough, all work in South Jungle came to a halt. If the packers couldn't pack, the pickers couldn't pick, and the sweepers had no reason to be up in the trees. All the South monks gathered around the conveyor belt. Furious Face hurried toward me. Of all the supes, she was the one who gave me the most trouble and the least respect. She looked like she was ready to launch into a big protest, but I launched her a look that very definitively said, "Back off, monk!" Furious Face stopped in her tracks, waiting to see what I would do next.

We just stood there for what seemed like forever until I finally announced, "I'm declaring a safety stand-down and stopping the packing line. Everyone, turn your equipment into the locker and go home for the day."

The monks all stared at me, jaws dropped, and did nothing.

"I don't want the packers to get hurt, so, please, everyone, go home."

They stood there.

"It's okay; it's on my authority."

"You don't have that authority," said one of the monks, sympathetically. "You're going to get in big trouble." Others agreed with him, adding, "You're going to cost the company big bucks," and, "Alpha's going to be furious," and, "Don't risk your job for us."

"It's all right," they insisted. "We'll keep packing while you go to headquarters to get the authority to stop the line."

This made perfect sense, but I refused. "No. I will not allow my monks to get hurt for no reason. Go home."

It was quiet for a moment. Then they began applauding. Furious Face looked absolutely furious but said nothing.

I realized that my monks truly believed I was on their side, which made them willing to suffer some pain on my behalf. But I wondered if they had picked the right side because they might be fired along with me, especially those who had spoken up. I was sure Furious Face was making a mental note of their names.

# CHAPTER TWENTY
## *No More Charts, No More Metrics*

Angry, uncertain, determined, and fearful, I swung off to headquarters to let them know I was not going to allow my monks to be injured on the defective new packing line.

When I got there, Connie, who has been Alpha's assistant forever, told me that Alpha and the other C-suiters were in the Quarterly Safety Meeting. "They're all at the meeting tree," she explained.

"Can you interrupt the meeting and get Alpha over here so I can talk to him?" I asked. I was really overstepping here; I knew I should go up the chain of command. But there was no time to waste. "We've got a big problem in South."

"Oh no," Connie said with a smile. "He doesn't like to be interrupted. But if you stand nearby, you can hear what's happening, and as soon as they're finished you can go in."

Burst in on C-suiters? That was kind of a scary thought! But I went over to the meeting and peeked in. Bored Monk was talking in his usual monotone: "And now we'll hear from Will from North Jungle Safety."

"It's not Will," said Safety Guy, a little peeved. "It's Bill. My name is Bill, and I'm not *from* North Jungle Safety. I'm *head* of North Jungle Safety."

"OK," said Bored Monk.

Safety Guy began running through the quarterly numbers for all the jungles—North Jungle, Berry Jungle, Precious Jungle, Short Jungle, Shady Jungle, Sour Jungle, and the rest. Nobody was paying any attention to him. Alpha was doodling on a pad, and from where I was standing I could see he was writing

"GGG"—which might have stood for Great Grove Goodies, our big competitor—over and over again, crossing it out each time. The other C-suiters were passing papers to each other, snacking, and otherwise ignoring the presentation.

I have to admit, it was pretty boring. Safety Guy raced through the figures for each jungle, giving numbers and percentages, medians and modes, bar charts and pie charts, scatter plots and density maps for all kinds of metrics. He stat-talked his way through the Safety Dress Time metric, Sting a Hazard metric, Droppage Rate metric for the Zigzag lines, and dozens more metrics for bites, falls, tail tug, lost worker days, production stoppages due to injury, and so on. Then he showed charts that compared the safety numbers with the numbers for production, product quality, returns, customer complaints, equipment reliability, and all kinds of other things. I couldn't follow it all, but it seemed clear that overall, PBPB had nothing to brag about. Company-wide safety was iffy and not improving, production was up in some jungles and down in others, customer complaints were rising for some jungles and falling for others, and so on.

After a while, I wondered why Safety Guy hadn't talked about South Jungle.

Just then he said, "Finally, I'd like to talk about South Jungle."

My heart sank. He saved us for last, and that couldn't be good.

"Something good is happening in South," he said. "Safety has been steadily improving for many months. Production is also rising, as is customer satisfaction, ready-to-ship time, and quality. And cost is dropping."

Alpha suddenly stopped doodling and looked right at Safety Guy. The C-suiters, who always followed his lead, instantly did the same. But Safety Guy stopped dead, midsentence, thinking he had said something wrong.

"Say that again about South," Alpha said. "Slower."

Safety Guy went through South's numbers again, speaking slowly and showing the charts more carefully this time. I still wasn't sure what all those numbers and charts meant, but the gist of it was this: South was the best jungle in PBPB!

Once again, Alpha interrupted Safety Guy. "Why is South outperforming all the other jungles?"

"There are many factors to consider . . ." Safety Guy began.

"Forget the numbers, forget the charts. What do *you* think is the difference? Pick the out the one thing that makes the most difference."

Safety Guy replied without hesitation. "It's Lucy, the Manager of South Jungle Production. I looked at the Annual Perception Surveys for all the jungles, measuring worker morale and perception of leadership support for safety and other issues. I don't usually talk about this, but they factor in perfectly with the South metrics. Let me show you these charts I prepared on . . ."

Alpha cut him off again. "No more charts, no more metrics. Tell me about Lucy." Then he added, imperiously, "Wait." Alpha turned to the COO and asked, "Is this the same Lucy you've mentioned before?"

The COO nodded. "Yes, sir."

"Continue," Alpha said to Safety Guy.

Safety Guy took a deep breath, then said, "The Annual Employee Perception Surveys show that the South monks trust and respect Lucy, more so than in any other jungle. They believe she cares about them, and they're willing to listen to her when she talks about safety. They also feel her Superintendent, Greg, cares about them. Of all the jungles, South was the only one that followed the Crush Guard initiative perfectly. That's because—and it's here in the Perception Surveys—Lucy gave a rollout speech that convinced the monks she cares about them. And there's something else. She came up with her own initiative for the sweepers, and she asked them to contribute their ideas for it. Now they think of that initiative as their own, as if they created it, and they follow it 100 percent. This is amazing because South has always had terrible Perception Survey results. Of all the jungles, the worst."

"What else?"

"Lucy and Greg go out together and talk to the monks once a week. They actually go out to the grove, into the trees and on the ground, to talk to monks as they're working. They have found a way to make the monks happy to see them and be willing to take their advice. If you let me plot this," Safety Guy continued, "I'm sure we'd see a direct relationship between perception and production."

"No more charts," Alpha growled. "Just get Lucy in here."

I blurted out, "I'm here!" and stepped in.

"You're Lucy," Alpha asked. Well, he sort of said-asked it.

"Yes, sir."

"Why were you standing there?"

If you're going to go picking high, I thought, might as well get 'em all while you're there. "There's a problem with the new packer belt in South, the one that was put in last night. It's installed improperly. The belt is too low, and the packers are going to strain their backs and legs."

"Get the owls to fix it."

"I can't. They're at their Hoo's-Hoo celebration."

"OK, I'll send over some repair monks."

"They won't know what to do. We need the owls, but they're not available until tomorrow. So," and I took a deep breath before saying this, "I stopped the packing line."

There was dead silence.

"I told the packers to go home. And the pickers and the sweepers. I shut down South Jungle, on my authority."

"You don't have that authority," said Alpha, in a surprisingly calm voice.

"No, sir, I don't. But I believe I have the authority to protect my workers and used that to close down the line."

Again, dead silence. Two dead silences in a row are really uncomfortable!

Finally, Alpha spoke. He said, to me, "Let's swing over to South."

And so we did.

## CHAPTER TWENTY-ONE
### *Who, Me? Really?*

Greg and Larry—that's the sweeper supervisor who likes coaching—were standing around in South Jungle by the packing line when they saw us swinging into South. So were a lot of the monks. They hadn't all gone home like I told them. A whole lot of them stayed and were talking, cleaning things up, and waiting for me to return—or to hear that I was fired. Greg later told me about his conversation with Larry, word for word:

"Hey," Greg said, nudging Larry. "There's Lucy, Alpha, and the whole C-suite swinging in."

"That can't be good," said Larry. "Look at how they're swinging with stiff arms, legs tucked, tails down. That's definitely bad. But why would they bring her back here to be fired? Why not can her at headquarters?"

"I don't know," answered Greg. "Make a public display of firing her? In front of all the South monks?"

Larry thought for a few moments, then said, "Here's a crazy idea: What if they're not going to fire her? What if she got permission to halt the line?"

"That's about 2 percent possible, but possible," Greg agreed. "But then why would they all be coming here? Management doesn't show up when things are going good. If Alpha and the whole C-suite are coming in, something really bad has happened." He paused for a moment, then continued. "Hey, you know what? Today was the Quarterly Safety Review at headquarters. South Jungle must have really bombed out, and now they're coming in to find out what went wrong and fire a bunch of us."

Larry, being newer and not as well versed in the way of big corporations, wasn't sure. "Maybe the review went well, and they're coming to see what went right."

Greg responded with one of the ruder sounds in the monkey lexicon, the one that means "what kind of %&@*% moron are you?"

Larry laughed.

"Management does *not* show up when things are going well," Greg said with certainty. "They're coming to chop off some tails. Lucy's and mine, for sure. Your best bet is to pretend you don't know us. And start kissing Furious Face's rump."

Just then, Alpha, the leadership team, and I landed. Greg knuckled over and stood next to me, as if to say, "I'm with her." Larry hung back and the rest of the monks, on the ground and in the lower branches, just watched.

Well, I thought, if I'm going to be fired, I might as well get a few of my ideas out. So I went over to the packer line, stepped onto the new walkway, and said, "See how I have to bend way over to pack? This was supposed to reduce strain and injuries, but it will increase them." I looked directly at Alpha as I continued. "I know safety's important to you. I've heard you say it many times. We've invested a lot of time and energy into making the monks safer. This will take us backward, which is why I called a safety stand-down and stopped the line." Now I looked him right in the eye and said, "You have said to us that safety is a big priority. Now tell me. Is it a big priority?"

There was dead silence. You could hear an ant drop.

As the silence continued, I found myself mentally calculating my pension. I had just vested a month ago, and with having only the bare minimum number of years and hours, I would get about 10 percent of my current salary but not starting until retirement age, which was a long way off. The Jungle Economic Commission had just passed that law saying you could take your pension with you when you went to a new company, but who would hire me now?

Finally, Alpha spoke. To me. "Let's knuckle," he said. The C-suiters stepped forward, ready to walk. "Not you," said Alpha, dismissively. "Just Lucy."

And so we knuckled, just him and me.

When we were a ways away from the others, Alpha began speaking. He spoke slowly, which was unusual, and he spoke calmly without a hint of impatience or anger, which was even more unusual. He said, "I began working in a small troop called Lovely Leaves. We picked and sold gourmet leaves to giraffes, gazelles, and other animals that live on the savannah. I never saw our customers; they were an abstraction to me.

"I began at the bottom as a packer. I had wanted to be a picker, or a sweeper as a second choice, but to be frank, I didn't have what it takes physically. After a couple years of packing, resentfully, I applied for a job in administration. It quickly became apparent that my abilities in administration more than compensated for my deficiencies in the trees.

"I moved up the ranks, entering the C-suite as COO. I was full of ideas, some good, some not so good, like replacing picker monkeys with leafcutter ants. That nearly cost me my job. Fortunately for me, the CEO retired for health reasons and, no other candidates being readily available, the leafcutter ant debacle was overlooked, and I became CEO.

"I decided that Lovely Leaves would become the largest company in the jungle, larger than Great Grove Goodies, larger than the Sloths' World of Leisure—and even better known than the Hyena House of Hilariousness. You may be too young to remember the House and how famous it was.

"I discovered that I had a talent for mergers and acquisitions, a flair for sniffing out a competitor's weakness and pouncing on it. Each new acquisition brought an opportunity for another, and so I focused on growing the company. We grew, diversified, and I changed the name to PBPB not long before we acquired your troop.

"I never acquire randomly or blindly. I always research carefully. I studied and wanted your troop specifically because of its reputation for risk-taking. I have but one child, a son. He has no desire to take over for me one day. He studied conflict resolution and has dedicated his life to bringing peace to the jungle. His dream is to create a jungle in which there are no predators, only pals.

"Having no heir, I thought I might find one among your troop of risk takers. In my position, you have to be fearless, sometimes reckless. You have to be a no-harness monk willing to leap without looking yet always land on your feet. That's the monk I wanted to take my place one day and continue growing PBPB until there are no competitors left to crush.

"I haven't found that monk. Instead, I've found you. Or perhaps it's more accurate to say that you've been dumped into my lap. And I'm not sure what to do with you."

We knuckled silently for a few moments. Then I said, hopefully, "Would you like to hear about my STEP team?"

He didn't answer, so I took that as a "yes" and launched into a description of my STEPers, the Sweeper Spotter initiative, focus, feedback, facilitation, and the other things Solophant had told me, and everything else I could think of.

We walked and I talked for quite some time.

## CHAPTER TWENTY-TWO
### *Alpha, Solophant and Me, Plus Phil*

It turns out that Alpha really does research things carefully—at least, things he cares about. That's why he insisted on meeting Solophant and learning about what I was learning. A few days later, as we were swinging out to see Solophant, Alpha asked me some questions:

"I've never heard of Solomon the Elephant," he said. "Has he founded or does he run a large company or institution?"

"Not that I know of," I answered.

"Has he made significant contributions to the science of business?"

"Not that I know of."

"Has he authored an important analysis?"

"Not that I know of."

"What do you know of Solophant?" Alpha asked, with just touch of sarcasm coloring his voice.

"He makes sense," I answered. "And my old boss trusted him."

Alpha thought for a moment. "Your old boss was Ted. I remember him. I crushed him."

"Well," I snapped back, surprised to find myself snapping at the big boss, "being good at crushing competition doesn't mean you're good at managing monks."

We continued on in silence. I wasn't surprised that Alpha didn't know who Solophant was because Alpha doesn't listen to outsiders or advisors. He doesn't pay any attention to anyone or anything but his gut instincts.

Luckily, Solophant was in, and, just as luckily, he was delighted to meet Alpha. "I have heard a great deal about you," Solophant said with a touch of admiration in his voice. "Your growth from Lovely Leaves to PBPB, overtaking Great Grove Goodies, is impressive."

"I apologize," replied Alpha, "for not taking the time to learn about you before dropping in. However, Lucy has informed me that you were an advisor to her former CEO, Ted, and have taught her a great deal about the science of managing monkeys with respect to safety issues."

"I prefer to think of it as the art of leadership," said Solophant, "touching all aspects of business. Lucy and I began with safety, for that that is what she was concerned about. But the approach to safety should be no different than the way one deals with improving quality, customer service, delivery, even production."

"I don't have time to deal with day-to-day safety matters," Alpha said, matter-of-factly. "I have a Safety Department to handle that. My focus in on running and growing the company."

"Let me ask you a few questions. First, is the head of your Safety Department a grunt, guardian, or guru?"

Alpha seemed puzzled. "What do you mean?"

"Where is the Safety Department positioned on your organizational chart?"

Alpha thought for a moment, then replied, a bit embarrassed, "I'm not sure."

"What is the name of the monkey who heads the Safety Department?"

Alpha did not have to think about that. "Once again, I'm not sure."

Solophant continued. "Can you recall reading a report from the head of the Safety Department? Can you recall a safety initiative created by the head? Can you recall sitting down to discuss matters with him or her?"

"No."

"Then the head of your Safety Department is a grunt, a paper pusher with no influence at all. And with no reason to go beyond distributing and collecting forms, creating quarterly and annual presentations to which no one pays any attention, and otherwise putting in time while waiting to retire.

"A step up from the grunt is the guardian. The guardian still works with the administrative, paperwork side of safety, but goes beyond. He oversees change implementation, always working to create a sense of ownership in safety initiative and ideas. He wants everyone, from worker to supervisor to superintendent, to feel as if they 'own' safety and truly care about it.

"At the top is the guru," explained Solophant. "A safety guru, whether she be in-house or an outside consultant, is a strategic thinker. She speaks directly to the top leaders, acting as a trusted advisor on all things safety. No matter what the status quo is, she continually challenges it and makes sure that safety strategy never competes with the business strategy; instead, they work together.

"It does not matter how many safety initiatives are launched, how many safety posters are hung about, how many observations or audits are conducted, or how many hours are spent training. You can tell precisely how much emphasis a company places on safety by asking the 'grunt, guardian, or guru' question. My second question to you is this: how far can a company that downplays safety grow before becoming mired down in injuries?"

Alpha bristled. "I would not agree that we've downplayed safety. We have simply emphasized other areas. We comply with all the safety regulations."

I smiled inside because I knew what was coming.

"You comply with all the safety regulations," Solophant said, nodding his head. "Yet your monks continue to be injured. And from what I hear, only one of your jungles has been able to move the needle on safety. That is Lucy's jungle, which goes beyond the regulations, to coaching."

"I concede the point," said Alpha, grudgingly. "I'm here to learn."

And learn he did, I have to admit. Alpha listened carefully as Solophant gave Alpha the same lessons he had given me:

> Every organization, no matter how large or small, requires leadership. There are many styles of leadership, including the vicious bullying of the lions, the monarchy of the ants and bees, the "two on top" of the wolves, the "grandma in charge" of the elephants, and the cooperative of the meerkats. All these leadership styles have their strengths and weakness and are appropriate for different enterprises and situations.
>
> The key is to find the style of leadership that produces the best results for your organization. For monkeys, with their desire for autonomy and mastery, their wish to feel

as if their efforts are appreciated and to contribute to something bigger than themselves, the most effective leadership approach is coaching.

Simply put, coaching is focusing on the behaviors that will lead to the best results, providing constant feedback when these behaviors are seen or not seen, and facilitating. Facilitating means helping to overcome the internal and external influences that make it difficult for monkeys to perform at their best.

Once you have decided upon coaching as the form of leadership, you have to decide what you are coaching your monks for. In PBPB's case, we are coaching for the HELP precautions. We want to help the monks learn why they need to focus on these behaviors to best accomplish their goals: give them continuous feedback on their efforts, successful and unsuccessful; facilitate their efforts to excel by giving the necessary tools, removing obstacles, and improving the safety systems to address the hazards as the work is performed; and continually look for new ways to apply the coaching/focus/feedback/facilitate formula in new areas. That is, if we begin by coaching for safety, we can later expand the same approach out to quality, customer service, and every other aspect of the organization.

The gist I just gave was brief, but Solophant went into great detail, spending hours talking, showing us articles from the *Jungle Business Review* and quoting stats from *Lily Pads*, which is a series of scholarly white papers published by the frogs.

The upshot of that lengthy conversation was that Alpha was persuaded to give coaching, focus, feedback, and facilitation a chance.

"We've already begun coaching and focus in South Jungle," he said as we swung back to headquarters.

"We?" I thought. "*We've* begun?

"Our initial efforts have been encouraging. But suppose something happens to you? How will our efforts continue?"

Since *our* initial efforts have been so encouraging, I thought, if something happens to me, *you* can continue them. That's what I thought but didn't say.

"I'll give you additional authority so you may continue coaching in South Jungle. You've begun focus. Experiment with feedback and facilitation but hold back on finding new results. We'll save that for later once we see how focus, feedback, and facilitation play out."

"How much authority do I have?" I asked.

"Three-quarters banana."

Three-quarters? That's pretty good! "OK," I said. "I'll begin by disbanding the Reminder Monks."

"Agreed," he said. "And I'll transfer them out of South. I'm sure many monks are too angry at them to work with them."

"Then," I continued, "I want to fire most of my supervisors, eight of the nine. They always give me trouble."

"No," said Alpha. "The most I will allow is firing or transferring out one supervisor. You must persuade the others to follow you. If coaching works so well, then coach them to your side. If you can do that, I'll be impressed."

"Agreed!" I said, though I had absolutely no idea how I would persuade all but one of my supervisors to join me. "And one more thing," I added. "We have to do something with the head of safety."

"Yes. What is his name?" Alpha asked, genuinely perplexed. "Will?"

"I keep thinking Phil," I answered, "but that doesn't sound right. Whatever it is, I'd like to see him upgraded from grunt and have him work with me on this."

"Agreed," said Alpha.

I wasn't sure what I'd do with Safety Guy, or if he was even interested in being upgraded. But I knew I didn't like having the Safety Department buried in North Jungle, and this was my chance to push it up the hierarchy a bit. Even if I totally failed and went back to picking, safety would be a little higher on the chart.

## CHAPTER TWENTY-THREE
## *Shall We Dance?*

As soon as I got back to South Jungle, I launched the "great experiment." That's not what it was called, but it's how I thought of it because I really didn't know what I was doing. I was making things up as I went.

First, I filled out the forms to get rid of the 'Minder Monks, transferring them out to different jungles so they wouldn't all show up in a single jungle and overwhelm it with their 'Minder mindset.

Second, I filled out the forms to get a few more monks in Safety Guy's department. They would handle most of the paperwork, freeing Safety Guy up to work on the guardian part of safety.

Third, I went to headquarters and looked in the files to see what Safety Guy's name was, once and for all. It's Bill.

Fourth, I went to Alpha's office, got him to sign off on the transfers, and told him that I was going to have Bill go with Greg and me on our Friday tours through South Jungle, learning about coaching, focus, and all that, and so he would be seen by the monks. Not just be seen but be seen as one who cares about the workers and wants to help them be as safe as possible. I would also ask Bill to keep notes on everything that happened, thinking I might use them later on. "I could do a seminar on coaching and the rest for management," I explained, "once I master it all."

Alpha agreed to everything and told me to report to him weekly.

The "great experiment" got off to a good start. Bill caught on quickly and soon began doing what he learned in North Jungle, as well. Greg, my superintendent, took over some of my paperwork so I could spend more time learning about, then doing, coaching.

And then, Greg and I went dancing. Actually, we went to see the All-Species Ballroom Dance Championship, which was only held once every four years and was *the* place to see the very best dancers in the world gliding through the waltz, tango, and other dances.

This was Solophant's idea. He told me that this year, the All-Species was going to introduce a new feature. After the preliminary and elimination rounds, the top five finishers would be given exactly thirty minutes to learn a brand new, very complicated dance, which they would perform in the championship round.

Each of the five couples would be assigned a dance teacher who would teach the couple the new dance. Only the most V of VIPs would be allowed to sit in and watch these teaching sessions. Solophant, who seemed to have connections everywhere, arranged for Greg and me to get passes.

"Pay close attention to the teaching styles," Solophant admonished before we left for the competition. "Notice carefully how each of the teachers provides feedback. This is a high-pressure situation in which the dancers must absorb a lot of information very rapidly. The type of feedback they receive will be crucial."

It was so exciting! The preliminaries and eliminations were incredible, and right from the start I could tell the flamingo couple was going to the finals. When they stretched out those long legs and wings for the waltz, they seemed to be flying across the floor—although actual flying was illegal, you had to keep your feet (or paws, or claws, of hoofs, or webs) on the floor at all times. And the way they intertwined their necks! I don't even know how to describe it!

    I also liked the polar bear couple, and they went all the way. They were so cute in their matching igloo hats, and for big animals, they moved very lightly.

As the finalists were announced, most everyone agreed that either the flamingos or polar bears would win. The other finalists were the ducks, the lions, and the camels. Just between you and me, I would not have picked the camel couple for the final round. I don't mean to criticize, but when I think ballroom dance, I just don't think "camel."

Still, Greg and I loved promenading under the red canopy to the teaching area where the five final couples were going to learn the "secret final dance," as the announcer called it. Waiters passed around with endless trays of delicious leaves, fruits, and other delicacies for the VIP guests, provided courtesy of PBPB and Great Grove Goodies. Greg and I ran from stage to stage, watching the teachers teach the dancers the dance.

The polar bears' teacher was quick to point out the slightest fault, and kept saying things like, "No! I said heel-toe, toe, toe-HEEL. It's toe-HEEL! Toe-HEEL! Toe-HEEL!" I don't know how to translate that ballroom lingo, but I sure caught the negativity in the teacher's tone.

The flamingos' teacher, on the other hand, was pretty quiet. She rattled off the steps, walked through a few figures to demonstrate, then mostly sat and watched as the flamingos practiced the dance numerous times.

The lions' teacher was full of advice, often interrupting the dancers to give them lengthy bits of instruction. I could tell by the lion's body language that they felt these interruptions were unwelcome and unnecessary because the advice offered was not well suited to their needs. Meanwhile, the duck couple's teacher seemed to be full of concern, constantly telling the ducks how much he wanted them to succeed. He repeatedly asked them if there were other ways they could see the figures being performed and said he was eager to provide a safe space for providing performance feedback.

But my favorite teacher was the one assigned to the camel couple. He was full of positive reinforcement, saying things like, "excellent heel release," "the pendulum motion was spot on," and "the commence to rise was perfect!" Again, I don't know what any of that means, but he was so encouraging!

All five finalist couples then went back to the dance floor for the final round. Each did the "secret final dance," and they were all incredible. But one couple stood head and hump above the others, and the winner was obvious: the camels! They nailed it. They nailed the steps, the musicality, the interpretation—everything. They got the top score in every category. As for the two couples everyone thought was going to duke it out for the championship, the flamingos finished fourth and the polar bears were dead last.

"The competition was your lesson in feedback," Solophant said when I went to see him the next day. "The dancers were equally adept at learning new material. The big variable was the teacher and, as you noted, each teacher is different. Each provides a different type of feedback that plays into the learning process.

"You must always remember," he continued, "that every single response from a teacher or a supervisor or manager is a form of feedback, a form of teaching. Spewing negativity is a form of feedback, as is absolute silence. Looking away and saying nothing is a form of feedback, as is constant carping, expressions of concern, and providing information. The weak can be lifted up by positive criticism while the very best can be destroyed by negativity, silence, and other unhelpful forms of feedback.

"Every single thing that you, as a manager, do or do not do is a form of feedback. Think carefully about the type of feedback you are providing and the manner in which you wish to offer it."

## CHAPTER TWENTY-FOUR
*Posterior for Posterity?*

The 'Minder Monks had been gone for a couple of weeks and none of the South Jungle pickers, packers, or sweepers missed them. Neither did they miss having to arrive early for work to put on all their safety equipment and then stand in line to be checked by stickling 'Minders who handed out notices for every little infraction.

"The Reminder Monks are examples of pure punishment," Solophant had explained to me. "You certainly need consequences for those who fail to exhibit the desired behavior. But punishment as the first and only form of feedback is not an effective approach for workers who are asked to exercise judgment."

The South Jungle monks still had to use their safety equipment and follow all the safety rules, but now they felt as if we trusted them to get it right. As I saw it, our job—mine, Greg's, and the supervisors'—was to help the workers master what they needed to know and do, supply occasional reminders, applaud them when they did well, and help them learn from their errors when they did not.

But if the workers were happy, the Supervisors were not. Stripped of their 'Minders and knowing that I had Alpha's support to make some big changes, the South Supervisors were rapidly losing their iron grip on South Jungle. They had heard that Alpha had given me permission to fire them all—actually, I could only fire one—so they were scared. A few of the supervisors tried to be nice to the workers, a few asked me for guidance, and a few avoided me. But not Furious Face. She seemed more determined than ever to continue her reign of terror.

The very next Friday, as Greg and I were going through South chatting with monks, we saw Furious Face chewing out a packer monk named London. We couldn't tell why; Furious Face seemed to be attacking London for six different infractions that happened at eight different times. And even though Furious Face saw us standing there and knew I didn't approve of this approach, she kept reproaching the poor monk. It reminded me of the polar bears' dance teacher saying, "Toe-HEEL, toe-HEEL, toe-HEEL!"

We watched her for a few moments and then Greg said to me, "You know, we're giving feedback right now."

"*I'm* not yelling at London," I replied, surprised.

"We're giving Furious Face feedback. Our silence is saying it's okay to be nasty to workers."

He was right. I had to do something right now. Solophant had said that expressing concern in a consistent and immediate manner is the most effective way to stop undesired behavior, which meant I should express concern to Furious Face over her undesired behavior. So I stepped into the fray, saying, "Good morning, London, Supervisor. Supervisor, there's an issue I'd like to discuss with you. Superintendent Greg will assist London."

Greg led London away, and I said to Furious Face, hoping I was getting this expressing concern thing right, "I'm glad you take such an interest in the jungle, and that you spend a great deal of time assisting the workers. I'm concerned about . . ."

"I'm not assisting," snapped Furious Face. "I'm correcting. That's what supervisors do, correct."

I tried again to express concern to Furious Face, but she wouldn't hear it. She interrupted again and practically snarled, "This is a workplace, not a nursery school. If the workers don't work the right way, I tell 'em what they did wrong. It's that's simple." With that, she turned and knuckled off.

Those were firing words! I could have given Furious Face her swinging papers right then and there, but I was still trying to figure this coaching thing out and I wanted to prove to Alpha I could make it work, even with the most difficult employees. So I decided to deal with this at a later time.

Greg and I spent a lot of time in South Jungle over the next couple of weeks, offering positive reinforcement when we saw monks demonstrating good behavior and expressing concern when they demonstrated undesired behavior. Then I'd gently probe to find out what we needed to fix, so they could be successful. For example, if we saw one monk helping another with a harness, we'd say, "It's great to see monks helping each other!" On the other hand, if we saw a monk doing something wrong, like attaching coconuts to the K2E pads so the rhinos would crack them, we'd take them aside and tell them we were concerned about their safety and performance.

We'd try to understand why these choices were being made and would ask if there was something we could do to help the monks follow the rules or take additional precautions. In the case of the coconuts, the "why" was so obvious I had missed it entirely! We used to have a nifty little coconut-cracker right by the packing belt, so the monks could open a coconut with ease. But when the cracker broke, we never replaced it, so monks began smacking coconuts with their helmets to open them, taking them high in the trees and dropping them, or attaching them to the K2E pads. Monks were making unsafe choices because they were used to having coconuts. Getting a new coconut-cracker for South Jungle solved the problem.

We also talked with the monks about the new balance of consequences for desired and non-desired performance that I had drawn up. In other words, what would happen if workers did what was desired, such as recognition and thanks for their contributions to improving safety? They were not used to receiving positive reinforcement, so our thanks were as appreciated as they were unexpected. I also made sure to remember that what one monk thought was a positive consequence might bug the heck out of another. Some monks, for example, loved being praised by management in front of their peers. But other monks would work really hard to *not* be singled out in front of the crowd.

Also, because I wanted to be transparent about setting expectations, I let them know what would happen if they did what was undesired. We had a series of graduated consequences for willful and repeat nonperformance, ranging from verbal warnings, to written warnings, to offering to help them find a new place of employment.

Over the next few months, the safety numbers steadily improved as we proactively addressed the obstacles and barriers to safe performance. Workers began following the safety rules out of habit, as if it was second nature to them. And more than once, I heard more experienced workers explaining things to new workers, saying things such as, "Think HELP: H for hands, E for eyes on path, L for line of fire, and P for position of your feet," then going on to explain what that means. I also saw more employees giving positive reinforcement to each other or expressing concern that a monk was taking a risk. Some of the conversations I overheard were pretty impressive. I could tell that many of the monks had moved past blaming and shaming and really understood the powerful influences that shape behavioral choices.

The only thing I wasn't happy about was Furious Face. She was not going to change her ways no matter how much concern I expressed. And she did not do anything on the plus side that would let me give her any positive reinforcement. We were at an impasse until "it" happened, with "it" being one of the more unforgettable accidents that ever happened in South Jungle. They're still talking about it today. Well, laughing about it more than talking about it. Here's what happened:

Furious Face was in the packing area when she saw a picker monk drop out of a tree. The picker hadn't descended to the appropriate level before dropping to the ground; he was a couple of feet too high up. Determined to give him a good scolding, Furious Face started knuckling over to him. But the long conveyor belt was in her way. If she went around it, she would lose sight of the miscreant monk, so instead, she got a running start and leapt up into the trees, intending to grab hold of a branch, swing around it once, then land on the other side of the conveyor belt. Unfortunately for her, the branch broke and instead of landing on her feet on the other side of the belt, Furious Face landed on her rump in a bunch of wet concrete that had just been poured to make a new walkway. When she stood up, all the monks started laughing at the perfect impression of her rear end in the concrete.

One of the braver monks grabbed a note pad and, pretending to be a 'Minder Monk, quickly wrote something on the pad, ripped off a sheet of paper and threw it at Furious Face. "Here's a warning notice for failure to stand within the jump zone before initiating a leap," he said.

Another monk grabbed a piece of paper and threw it at her, saying, "Here's a 'Retraining Required' notice for not filling out 'Form 123—Swinging on a Branch That's Too Thin to Hold Me.'"

Meanwhile, London measured the imprint of Furious Face's rump in the cement and announced, "Largest rump circumference ever recorded in South Jungle cement!"

Another monk stood right by the rump impression, pointed to it and announced, in a very grand voice, "This artwork is entitled, 'Posterior for Posterity'."

The ever-growing crowd of monks let out a cheer and some of them decided that they, too, should imprint their rumps for posterity, so they hopped up onto the conveyor belt and leapt, posterior first, into the wet cement.

The merriment continued as the South monks let out years' worth of anger and frustration on Furious Face who was, for once, absolutely powerless. And totally humiliated.

I really wish I had been there to see it. Actually, now that I think of it, no. If I had been there, I would have had to stop it. But I doubled over laughing when I heard about it and really had to struggle to keep a straight face when Furious Face came to see me after cleaning up.

"I hope you're happy," she said. "You've got your reason to fire me."

I was indeed very happy but not because I could fire her for breaking a bunch of safety rules. I had longer vines to swing on. Much longer. If I could convert my biggest opponent to my way of thinking, I could do anything.

So I said to Furious Face, "The way the monks responded to your, um, incident, was inappropriate. But their behavior is a direct result of your behavior because this is the culture you created for them—and with them. Your actions help determine what they think, what they do, and how they perceive the importance of safety compared to production.

"The way you've been leading is just not acceptable. And it will change, now. I believe you can make the change. But I need to do a better job setting clearer expectations and ensuring that you have the skills to be the type of leader we need here. And I could do a better job of holding you accountable for creating the culture that we need to be safe and competitive. I need to show you the way. Will you let me coach you?"

Astonished, Furious Face stammered, "You, you're not going to fire me?"

I let her know that everyone makes mistakes, especially in complex environments, and I wanted to give her an opportunity to be a better leader. She lowered her head, and I saw a look in her eyes that told me I had gotten through to her. Things would be different going forward in South Jungle, I just knew it!

# CHAPTER TWENTY-FIVE
## *Rump Pizza and an "Innovation of Interest"*

The months flew by, and soon I was doing a lot of stuff above my manager position. In addition to my duties in South, I was going to all the other jungles—North Jungle, Precious Jungle, Berry Jungle, Shady Jungle, Short Jungle, NN Jungle, Buzz Jungle, and the rest—talking with the managers and supervisors about coaching, focus, feedback, and more. And I'd go with them to the packing areas and into the trees, showing them my approach to connecting with workers, getting to know who and what was important to the individual monks, giving feedback, and more.

I also encouraged the other managers to set up their own STEP teams. They were all enthusiastic about STEP because they knew about South Jungle's increasingly impressive stats. In fact, several managers asked if they could borrow my STEPers, but I said no: each jungle had to have its own team, made up of monks from that jungle, who knew that jungle's culture, were receptive to change, and were respected by the workers in that jungle. I did, however, ask Ozzie, a really bright member of my STEP team, to go and talk to each new STEP team as it formed, giving them the benefit of his experience.

All of this kept me really busy, so Superintendent Greg took over a lot of my manager work. This meant he was super busy, so Supervisor Larry started doing some of Greg's superintendent stuff, and Ozzie began assisting Larry. I thought this was great: The next wave of South Jungle leaders was being trained.

Meanwhile, I continued working with Furious Face. She was my big test case. I thought that if I could coach her to be a good supervisor, I could coach any monk. I began by having her go with Greg and me on our regular Friday "get to know the monks tour" through South Jungle and made it a point to stress to her how a good supervisor helps ensure that the workers had the necessary training, attitude, and ability to do great work and that management was not getting in their way by setting up obstacles or contrary influences.

But it was hard going for poor Furious Face because so many of the monks hated her. They called her "Supervisor Rump-Rump," sometimes right to her snout. And when they saw her coming, they'd chant "rump-rump, rump-rump" to warn the others. It was humiliating for her, but she stuck to it with the same intensity she had shown in the past, only now in a positive way.

She even tried to show her picker monks how much she had changed by bringing pizza when she called a meeting for safety or some other issue. She spent a lot of her own money to get the really pricy Elephant Pizza, which, as the ad said, had "tons of tasty-terrific toppings." But the pickers refused to bite into what they referred to as "Rump Pizza."

At first, Furious Face needed a whole lot of feedback, the kind you use to change bad behavior to good behavior. Sometimes, the problem was her tone or choice of words. Something as simple as vocal volume or showing empathy can make one monk feel appreciated but a second monk offended. When I saw things like this, I would express concern to Furious Face and ask how what she had just said would improve her relationship with the monk and how would it help create the teamwork South Jungle needs to be successful. And I wouldn't let her ignore a situation. If I saw Furious Face swinging by a monk who was doing something risky without saying anything, I would remind her that silence was a form of feedback. "The monk knows you saw that behavior," I would say to Furious Face. "So not saying anything is actually saying to the monk that it's okay."

Over time, she started thinking of her role as helping the monkeys do their job by coaching them, and I could start giving her positive reinforcement feedback. I wish I had something dramatic to tell you about her, like she single-handedly battled three giant snakes to protect a wounded picker, but I don't. Furious Face just worked at getting better, and little by little, month by month, she did. And finally, I saw her having a really constructive interaction with one of her picker monks:

Furious Face caught the picker, whose name was Charlotte, using homemade equipment up in the trees. This is strictly forbidden. Worse yet, Charlotte was using her homemade thing on the Zigzag lines, and tampering with the lines could cause the whole thing to crash down and maybe injure a lot of monks on the ground. But rather than scold and threaten, Furious Face asked the monk why she was using homemade equipment. Charlotte said her device solved the problem of transferring the buckets of fruit and leaves from one line to the other—a problem that had plagued us from Day 1. She had been using it, on the sly, for months now, "And it works!"

In the old days, Furious Face would have belittled Charlotte, mockingly calling her a genius, threatening to fire her, and slapping her with fines. But now she actually had a conversation with Charlotte. She began by reminding Charlotte of the need to follow the safety rules for everyone's protection. Then she asked the picker to demonstrate her device. Charlotte did, and it seemed to solve the problem of falling buckets. So Furious Face again reminded Charlotte of the need to follow the rules, asked Charlotte to come to her if she had any other ideas for improvement rather than using them on the sly, and promised to write up a report on the Zigzag transfer device right away.

The next day, Furious Face handed me a report on an "innovation of interest" with a recommendation that the Tech

Department look into it. I was delighted! I said to her, "The way you spoke with Charlotte was exactly the right way to handle the situation. You recognized that she broke the rules for a reason. But there was no ill intent; she was trying to solve a problem. And we want monks like her, the workers, to help us solve problems because they're closest to the problems. They deal with these things every day, so of course they're going think about solutions. As supervisors, and managers, and leaders, we have to spend a lot more time listening to our workers. In this situation, you listened, you reminded her of the importance of safety rules, and you appreciated her ingenuity. You gave her an experience that will encourage her to be creative—but more appropriately so in the future. Thank you. That is exactly the type of leadership we need around here."

I passed the report on to Tech. They looked at it, said the device was pretty good, and asked if I would allow Charlotte to transfer to the Tech Department. Charlotte was flattered by the request, so off she went.

And there was another bit of personnel news that really made me happy: Aaron was back! He had spent months and months working furiously at his physical therapy and was now applying that same energy to his new job in the North Jungle Safety Department. Aaron was officially a paperwork monk because he still had some difficulty getting around, but he asked to be sent out to talk to the monks about safety. "They'll listen to me," he said, "I got a lot of tree cred."

And the monks did pay attention when he spoke, partially because his attitude was so upbeat. When they asked him why he wasn't bitter about the accident and not being able to pick anymore, he would shrug and say, "That's the way the vine swings."

## CHAPTER TWENTY-SIX
### *North, Short, Shady, and Berry*

I was knuckling with Alpha on one of my "get to know the monks" tours, this one in Buzz Jungle. To my surprise, he had really gotten into coaching, particularly giving feedback. Unfortunately, he was definitely not a natural like Greg. When he talked to a worker, it always seemed like he was reading from a script and the words were in a language he didn't understand. I thought his mingling with the monks was going to be a disaster, but most of the workers really appreciated his effort. To receive an "atta monk" from him or, even better, a Coach Coin, was considered quite prestigious.

We were knuckling through Buzz when Alpha said, "My father always told me that no one owes you a job. You have to work for it and work hard. That was 100 percent true when I was starting out, and it is 100 percent true now. Well, I owe you something, and I'm going to redeem that debt in the form of a promotion. As of now, you are Vice President of Improvement."

My first thought was, "WOW, that's great!"

My second thought was, "What's Vice President of Improvement?"

My third thought was, "Is he kicking me upstairs to get rid of me?"

Before I had time for a fourth thought, Alpha continued. "Your job will be to do what you've been doing but at a very high level. Guru-level. You won't be under any of the C-suiters. You'll report directly to me, weekly."

"OK," I replied, "but how about if my title is 'Vice President of *Continuous* Improvement?'"

"Why add 'continuous'?"

"Because we should never be satisfied with where we are. We shouldn't think that we're perfect and have nothing else to do."

Alpha was about to speak, but I hurried on, "Even if we get great safety numbers and production and profit numbers, things don't stay the same over time. Our employees change, our customers change, our products change, our technology changes, our locations change, our competition changes—everything changes. What worked perfectly for us today may not be so good tomorrow. And we change too, you and I. Our ideas evolve. We come up with better ways to do the same things. We should never be satisfied, which is why I should be Vice President of Continuous Improvement."

Alpha agreed. We finished up our "get to know the monks tour" of Buzz, and I swung back to South Jungle to get things ready. I talked to Greg, Larry, and Ozzie, and we agreed that Greg would take my place as Manager, South Jungle Production; Sweeper Supervisor Larry would take Greg's place as Superintendent; and Ozzie would become a Sweeper Supervisor. Ozzie said he should resign from the STEP team because having a supervisor on the team might make the other STEPers reluctant to speak up at meetings.

"Yeah, that makes sense," I thought. "Our culture still isn't very trusting." So I agreed with Ozzie, filled out all the paperwork, and swung back to headquarters as quickly as possible to get Alpha's sign-off. When I gave him the forms, he handed them back to me and said, "Don't ask my permission anymore. Strategize with me and then do what you feel needs to be done."

And so I did. I moved the Safety Department out of North Jungle and put it right beneath me on the organizational chart. So now Bill reported to me, and I reported to Alpha, which meant that safety issues and ideas had a short and direct route to the top. And I brought Bill with me to occasional leadership meetings—in addition to those at which he gave the stats—so everyone would see how much I valued him.

I now spent much of my time out in the jungles, talking about and doing coaching. It took some time, but most of the managers and supervisors of the various jungles caught on to coaching, and some were pretty good at it. As Solophant explained to me when I went to tell him of my promotion and learn more about coaching, "There are five reasons for undesired performance or lack of desired performance. They are that the monkey is unwilling, unable, unaware, or unaccountable, or the desired performance is drastically unlike the organizational culture."

"So what was, or what is, Furious Face? It took a lot of coaching, but she switched over."

"Furious Face was a combination of unaware and unaccountable. She is obviously willing to improve, according to what you have told me of her present behavior. However, in the past, no one made it their mission to spend the necessary time to explain to her precisely the type of leader needed and how she could become that leader. She is becoming more aware as you coach her, and if you continue to hold her accountable for these behaviors, she will thrive."

"How about Larry?"

"Is Larry the supervisor who seemed interested in coaching but hung back?"

"Yes. What's he?"

"Larry also appears to be willing and likely possesses innate ability and awareness of what was needed. However, he was being held accountable for other organizational priorities, such as production and strict discipline. He was skilled in paying attention to what his boss was paying attention to, which was production. As your focus has matured and you are holding him accountable for other priorities, he too will do well. Always remember that you must continually coach for the desired behavior or behaviors. Your organizational priorities change on occasion, and positive reinforcement is hardly overused in an operation. Ask yourself, Lucy, have you ever grown sick and tired from all the positive feedback you get at work?"

"Nope! I love praise as much as the next monk. But what about monks who don't fit the organizational culture?" I asked. "We have different cultures in the different jungles, and the whole company is shifting culture. How do I deal with monks who are unlike the many different cultures in PBPB, especially when we don't know where we'll wind up with all this change we're doing?"

"Tell me about the different cultures."

"Well, North Jungle, where I started, has a bare-knuckle, chest pounding culture. They pride themselves on ignoring the rules or breaking them, yet still producing a lot.

"Short Jungle is, well, I'd say it's like a family. They pick from bushes, not tall trees, so the monks stand on the ground or not very high up on ladders. Safety isn't much of an issue because there's not a lot that can go wrong there. And when something goes wrong, the supervisors run over to hug the worker who goofed up and say, 'Don't worry, we'll figure this out.'

"You already know about South Jungle. Then there's Shady Jungle, which is a mess because even in the daytime, it's dark there. And it's really rainy, so with all the darkness and dampness, the foliage grows wild, the spiders and snakes there are more dangerous than in any other jungle, and everything rots pretty quickly: Machinery, safety equipment, branches, everything rots. They've always been the jungle with the worst stats, and they think of themselves as being the biggest losers in PBPB. I've seen monks cry when they hear they're being transferred to Shady."

I continued explaining the cultures in Berry Jungle, NN Jungle, Buzz Jungle, and the rest.

When I finally stopped blabbing, Solophant said, "It is quite common for organizations to have different cultures in different departments or locations. That is why you must begin with an understanding of what success looks like to you—that is, your vision for a great operation—and then assess where the culture, systems, and structure stand today, both for the overall operation and for the individual units.

"In my travels and conversations with leaders, I have learned that every culture wants to feel unique. Indeed, they are unique, for they are made up of a unique group of animals facing a unique combination of the same challenges the other groups in the organization face.

"What will be truly unique is how you help them execute on improvement. What has worked with one group might fail with another due to the composition of the group; their attitudes toward themselves, their work, and the organization; and their experiences with successful and failed change efforts in the past.

"Not everyone will wish to be a part of your vision. You will need to discover each individual's inclination for yourself, help them understand the direction things need to go, have the confidence and competence to do what is required to get them there, and hold them accountable with a balance of frequent and consistent consequences—positive and negative—along the way.

"You can accomplish this with coaching, despite the disparate cultures within PBPB. Properly used, coaching is a superior style of leadership to help groups move from poor to good and from good to excellent."

"OK. And what about those who are absolutely unwilling?"

"Do your best to help them adopt the desired behavior. If they refuse to evolve, politely escort them to the exit."

# CHAPTER TWENTY-SEVEN
## *And Finally, Facilitation*

Fortunately, there was a lot less exit-escorting than I would have thought. All across PBPB, less than a dozen supervisors and managers proved to be absolutely unwilling or unable to change their ways, despite constant, timely feedback. And only a couple dozen worker monks were absolutely unchangeable.

"Those numbers are typical," said Solophant when I finally found time to visit him again. "In very few cases, a monk is unable or unwilling to change due to personal factors. In most cases, however, a monk's behavior is a product of the environment, process, and systems that they work within; the tools available to him or her; and the perceived pressure and priorities. And this brings us to facilitation. Your efforts at coaching, focus, and feedback have been remarkably successful. But you've spoken of issues that you could not resolve because you lacked the authority. Now that you are Vice President of Continuous Improvement, you can work on handling these larger or more systematic problems through facilitation."

"That's dealing with obstacles and barriers, right?"

"Yes. It can also mean enabling the desired perceptions or habits. Having spent a great deal of time speaking with and observing the monkeys, you have learned that workplace behavior is rarely random. Monks do things for a reason. The reasons for deviation from a desired outcome are often complicated, which means you must do more than simply 'fix' the worker in question. Workplace behavior is largely shaped by the workplace environment, which may encourage the monks to be their best, their worst, or something in between. Your next step, facilitation, is to discover how you can make it easier for them to perform reliably at their highest level. Go speak to and observe the monks again, asking yourself what is influencing their behavior and whether changing those influences will change their behavior for the better. Always remember that they may not be aware of these influences."

"OK," I replied, doubtfully. Doubtfully, because I didn't know how I could figure facilitation out. If a monk was unaware of what was driving him, how was I to know? But I had learned a lot by talking to and watching monks before, so I went back to talking and watching. I had always been bothered by Machine Monk Max's fall, minor as it was, so I began by talking to him. I asked why he was—and why he still is—dashing madly, and blindly, across the branchwalk several times a day.

"I have to get the boxes of oil cans," he explained when I went out to see him. "Can't run the belt without oil. But I can't leave the control panel for very long, either. If I do, the conveyor belt will get out of sync. Or maybe I'll miss some stress fracture readings on the trees."

"The trees the rhinos are crashing into?" I asked.

"Yes," he nodded. "The trees are pretty strong, but nothing is really rhino-strong. I'd been getting some bad readings for a few days, so the day of my accident, I was really watching the stress readings. Didn't want to leave my panel much."

"I appreciate your diligence," I said with a smile. "So tell me, why do you have to keep getting the boxes of oil cans?"

"They're only delivered one box every half hour."

"Why is that?"

"A long time ago, someone from headquarters figured out that I use about a box every half hour. So that's what they give me. One every half hour."

Aha! A chance to facilitate. "Suppose all the boxes for the day were delivered at once? Would that make your job easier?"

"No. See, I can only stack so many boxes by my panel. I'd still have to run back and forth to get the rest."

That made sense. "So tell me, why are the boxes put on the branch-walk so far away from you?"

"Way back when I started, we had a different configuration for the assembly line. Actually, that's a couple of configurations back. A lot of the branch-walk ran right over the conveyor line, so you couldn't get to the control panel to give me the boxes. You had to put them down at the end of the branch-walk. That was okay back then, 'cause the branch-walk wasn't that long. But then we brought in the rhinos and K2E pads, and the branch-walk got a whole lot longer. All Delivery knew was that they should put the boxes at the end, so that's what they did, even though the end is now really far away from me."

"But the area around your control panel is easy to access today. It's been that way ever since I can remember."

"I've said that to the supervisor many times."

"Would it help if the boxes were delivered to you at the control panel? Not all at once but periodically through the day?"

"Sure would."

I wasn't sure how do to that, so I mentioned it to Greg, who was now Manager of South Jungle. He checked out the branch-walk, chatted with Max, figured out how many boxes could be safely stacked by the control panel, talked with Delivery, and arranged to have half-a-days' worth of boxes stacked by the control panel before Max arrived for work. The rest were brought in several hours later—and they were brought right to Max at his control panel.

Problem solved! Or maybe I should say, solution facilitated! Not only was Max safer because he didn't have to run blindly anymore, but Delivery was happier because they only had to make two trips a day instead of one every half hour.

Thinking back to the five reasons monks do things, I realized Machine Monk Max had been doing risky things because he was unable to do otherwise. And he was probably unaware of the risk because he had been racing blindly across the branch-walk for years and had never had an accident, so he figured it was safe. But as Solophant had told me many times, not getting hurt doesn't mean that what you're doing is safe. That's false. At-risk behavior is at-risk behavior, and you don't need an accident to prove it.

Then I thought about the Maintenance Monk who put the wet paintbrush on the branch-walk, causing Machine Monk Max to go flying. His name was Lloyd. I read the accident report again and arranged to talk with him. "The report says you were wearing your painter's apron, and I remember you were 'cause I was there. Why didn't you put the wet brush in your apron?"

"Because we had the new ones," Lloyd said. "The new aprons. The old ones were leather, and waterproof. The new ones are thin cloth. Paint goes right through 'em. So we Maintenance Monks don't like to put wet paintbrushes in there. It's hard to get that paint out of our hides. That's why I put the brush on the branch-walk. Sorry." I told him there was no need to apologize. Instead, I thanked him, explaining that his honest feedback was exactly what we needed. Now I could better deal with an issue that might cause a monk to deviate from the desired behavior.

I looked into it and found out that Alpha had ordered the cloth aprons as a cost-cutting measure. I also found out that several other accidents had happened because Maintenance

Monks were not putting wet brushes in their cheap aprons. I wrote up orders to go back to the leather aprons and then shared the problem and solution with the Maintenance Monks. Another solution facilitated!

How about some more things to facilitate? Furious Face had tried leaping over the South Jungle conveyor belt, and a few monks were still leaping over and sliding under long belts in other jungles. Was it possible to build a bridge or branch-walk over some of those belts? And feasible? I didn't know, so I had Bill look into it.

How about the deluge of safety and performance initiatives? Do they make it easier for monks to perform at the highest level? Or just confuse them with change after change?

How about all those forms that supervisors fill out but no one reads? Do they make it easier for supervisors to perform at the highest level, or does it tell them that their job is a joke? And are we improving their performance by not training them to be supervisors? My coaching has helped a lot, but is it efficient and effective for me to teach them, one at a time, the supervisor basics? Couldn't we have seminars for all new supervisors?

And while we're at it, couldn't we be very clear and purposeful about the type of leadership and specific competencies we need? Couldn't we then hire for what we want or develop what we need before they start developing bad habits out in the groves?

How about the constant transfers in and out of certain jungles? Is that helpful or harmful?

How about having so many safety rules that no one even knows what they are, let alone being able to follow them? And how about all the safety equipment pickers and sweepers are supposed to wear? Which equipment is really helping the monks be their best, and what was getting in their way?

There were so many "how abouts," it took a couple of years to work through them, get rid of a lot of obstacles and barriers, change perceptions and habits, improve systems and controls, and introduce things that made it easier for the monks to perform at their best. Luckily, there was a lot more chatter between workers and management now. The workers gave us a lot of feedback along the way, and we did a lot more listening, which made everything a lot easier and made the changes we implemented more resilient and lasting.

As for culture, each jungle retained its unique culture through all the change, but now the cultures embraced safety. North Jungle was still highly competitive, but now the monks competed as a team to make North the jungle with the best production *and* safety culture. Short Jungle is still like a family, but now everyone thinks about how to keep the family members safe on and off the tree. Each jungle has embraced safety in a different way, to a different degree, and I am learning how to work with the various cultures for continual improvement instead of against them.

And I did one little thing to remind myself that we're always looking to improve. Whenever we set a goal for safety, production, or whatever, we don't call it "the goal." Instead, we call it "the next goal."

That's because we've stopped searching for perfection which, anyways, the monks never bought into. Instead, we are in continual pursuit of excellence. Monks will make mistakes, especially in complex environments, but that doesn't mean we will ever stop trying to be excellent. We're keeping the monks involved. We're creating a culture based on caring for each other, on observation, feedback, and facilitation by looking at what influences a worker to deviate from desired outcomes. We're being proactive, not reactive, and the monks are buying into the idea that we can get better one day at a time, proactively.

Here at PBPB, we call this Create Ownership and Change Happens (COACH)™.

# CHAPTER TWENTY-EIGHT
## *Pilot? Visionary?*

I am truly the luckiest monkey in the world!

My goal when I started as a picker was to serve everyone in the jungle. And now, as the newly appointed CEO of Plant-Based Premium Bites, I can help ensure that the thousands of monks working for PBPB are enabled and inspired to do the same.

Things are in pretty good shape. The various jungles are doing well with coaching, and I spent the last couple of years facilitating for the entire company as VP of Continuous Improvement. Our safety stats are better than they've ever been, and way better than those of our big competitor, Great Grove Goodies. Our production numbers are strong, as are the stats for product quality and returns, customer complaints, and everything else. Even the perception surveys are way up. News of all this has really spread, thanks to good press we've been getting from the Jungle Stock Exchange. Because of that, some of the best talent in the industry is starting to knock on our branch, asking about openings in our leadership ranks.

There are problems, of course, the biggest of which is the huge debt Alpha ran up M&Aing and the big strain on our budget. And I still have to coach the existing leadership team members who remain stuck in the old ways. But my very first act as CEO was to promote Bill to VP of Continuous Improvement and move him into the C-Suite. Then I promoted Aaron to take Bill's place as Head of Safety. Both Bill and Aaron are really big on coaching and both will report directly to me, which means I won't have to worry about underlings filtering the information I receive or mixed messages coming from the top.

Greg has been doing a great job as Manager of South Jungle. Its culture has slowly shifted since he took charge, set clearer expectations, coached, and held his leaders accountable to those expectations. Meanwhile, Larry, who was a strong Superintendent for Greg, recently transferred out of South to become Manager of Round Jungle, the newest one Alpha had set up, and Ozzie is now Superintendent in Sour Jungle. Other protégés of mine have been promoted in different jungles, so I've got helpers at every level, from supervisor to C-suiter.

Alpha, who retired to help launch his son's "Pals, Not Predators" program, really supported me during the transition, going with me to all the jungles to meet the workers, talking about how helpful I've been to him and how he's confident I'll be a great CEO.

All is well—wonderful, actually. I'm having a great time going through all the congratulatory Cheetagrams and gifts I've received—even one from the head of Great Grove Goodies!

Oh, here's a Cheetagram from Solophant! It says, "Dear Lucy, congratulations on your richly deserved promotion to CEO of PBPB. You have worked hard and learned much over the past several years, which is why I am confident that you will be a superb leader. Up until now, you have focused exclusively on intracompany affairs. Now you must, in addition, direct your gaze outward and take up the complex tasks of serving as the company visionary and pilot, dealing with customers, competitors, and the ever-changing economic conditions of the jungle. Should you require advice, I am here to help you."

What?

*I'm* the company pilot? The visionary dealing with ever-changing economic conditions of the jungle?

Uh-oh!

## ABOUT THE AUTHOR

Shawn M. Galloway is the CEO of ProAct Safety. He is a consultant, professional speaker and author of several bestselling books on safety strategy, culture, leadership and employee engagement. Leaders have embraced his principles and teachings among the best safety-performing organizations within every major industry. He is a columnist for several magazines and one of the industry's most award-winning and recognized prolific contributors.

www.ingramcontent.com/pod-product-compliance
Lightning Source LLC
Chambersburg PA
CBHW070448090426
42735CB00012B/2485